LISTEN & LIVE

Through the Gospel of John

CARI JENKINS

APG

Scriptures are taken from the NEW INTERNATIONAL VERSION (NIV): Scripture taken from THE HOLY BIBLE, NEW INTERNATIONAL VERSION ®. Copyright© 1973, 1978, 1984, 2011 by Biblica, Inc.™ Used by permission of Zondervan.

ISBN 978-1-947051-07-2 (paperback)
     978-1-947051-08-9 (Epub - ebook)
     978-1-947051-09-6 (MOBI - ebook)

Published by Armory Publishing Group, LLC.
10 W. Dry Creek Cir, Littleton, CO 80120.
www.armorypublishing.com

Illustrations by Robert Riester
Editing by Melissa Hicks
Design (interior and cover) by Mike Riester

Armory Publishing Group, LLC titles may be purchased at www.armorypublishing.com and in bulk for educational, business, fundraising, or promotional use. For information, please email info@armorypublishing.com.

Library of Congress Control Number: 2018954833

Printed in the United States of America

22 21 20 19 18   2 3 4 5   JS3000

Contents

To the First Ladies of the Pasadena White House

With special thanks to Ron and Denae,
who seek to hear God's voice and respond
with their lives in beautiful ways.
Also, special thanks to L'Interdit in Altea, Spain,
for the hospitality as I put it together.

Preface

As I set out to write, I struggled to put into words what I have been taught in my own time with the Father. It is through relationship with Him that I have learned, have been led, and have been transformed. I believe that God desires to form each of us and desires that we, you and I, would seek first His Kingdom and His way, knowing that in doing so we will have all we need to navigate the dynamics of this life.

So, instead of teaching what I have learned, I thought it would be best to share what I have heard and invite you to listen right along with me.

I believe that one of the greatest gifts of relationship with God is found in His desire to be in communication with us. More than any other voice, it is His that shapes, loves, and leads us to that which is good, beautiful, and true. Learning to listen and to respond with our lives is a deep joy.

There will be words in this book that you respond to with your heart and there will be some with which you will wrestle: both, I believe, are important responses.

Introduction

Listen and Live began as a personal journey through the book of John
using the Benedictine practice of Lectio Divina, or Divine Listening.
It is a way, practiced for centuries now, of listening for the voice of God as scripture is read.
The practice in short follows this pattern:

✢ Sit in silence.

✢ Read the passage and sit in silence again for one minute.

✢ Read the same passage a second time, followed by silence and the question, "Is there a word or phrase that stands out to you as you read?" Again, sit for one minute of silence.

✢ Read the passage for a third time, followed by silence and the question, "Is there a picture, idea, emotion, or thought that accompanies the word or phrase as you sit in silence?" Sit in silence for two minutes.

✢ Read the passage a fourth and final time. Sit for three minutes of silence and ask the question, "Is there an invitation for you in the passage for the next week?"

As you read, I encourage you to listen to the voice of God in the words of the text. My prayer for you is, that you will listen and live in response to what you read and hear. Treat this book as an ongoing conversation with God. Write your thoughts and prayers in the space provided. Record the people and circumstances that come to mind as you are invited to live out the truth heard. May you be blessed in your reading, listening, and living.

Using this Book

As you read the words that fill the following pages, be alert and ask Jesus to speak to you.

1. Before you read ask Jesus to speak to you through the passage.

2. Read the Scripture provided and sit in silence. What stands out to you from the text? A word? Thought? Feeling?

3. Read the following text. Is there anything that resonates, stands out or causes discomfort? Take those reflections to the Lord.

4. In the space provided, write what you hear from the Lord for your life.

5. Next ask the Father, "Is there an invitation for me in the Scripture?"

6. Write it down.

7. Read "A prompt for living." Who or what comes to mind? Write those things down.

8. Make note of what you are learning along the way.

9. Let this be a journey of learning to listen and respond with your life to the voice of your Good Shepherd.

JOHN 1 (Readings 1–17)

LISTEN
John 1:1-3

¹ In the beginning was the Word, and the Word was with God, and the Word was God. ² He was with God in the beginning. ³ Through him all things were made; without him nothing was made that has been made.

Nothing was made apart from my Word. My Word is continuing to speak through all created things. My Word does not go out and return void. My Word will continue its work until it is complete in every way. Creation itself is evidence of my Word, and creation itself is speaking as the waves crash, the wind blows, the sun rises and sets, the stars appear, the grass grows, and all living creatures give birth without prompting.

There is nothing but My Word that speaks life and order into existence, and their way is evidence of My Word at work.

You are an expression of My Word. You have been created on purpose, and it is good. Your life, the ease with which you breathe, the air that filters through your lungs and feeds your body, the ability of your eyes to open, and the way your heart beats are My Word at work in you. For in My Word all things are held together.

My dear child, you hold within you, My very Word. Do you see it? Accept that it is true and your whole life will change. My ever-present Word accompanies you through life and will complete the work of life in you.

What do you hear?

LIVE

How will you respond?

A prompt for living

Take a look at the world around you. What do you see? What evidence of Jesus, the Word of God, do you notice in those around you? In creation? Do something to encourage or speak of the life you see in those around you or share a story of how you have seen the Word of God in creation with a friend or family member.

LISTEN

John 1:4-5

⁴ In him was life, and that life was the light of all mankind.
⁵ The light shines in the darkness, and the darkness has not overcome it.

Life. Light.

These two words are expressions of me. They are constant reminders of my presence. They are powerful and hold only truth.

My very life is the light of humankind.

I am your light.

You know life. You know light.

You can tell when you walk in it and you know deep in your core when you walk against it. You know when your heart beats life through your veins, and you feel the suffocating compression of death as it forces itself upon you.

I have come that you might have life.

I have come that you would know light. Like the sun shining warmly, blanketing you with its inviting presence, so my light warms and invites you to all things good.

I am light. Darkness does not understand light. Nor does it over power it. You see my child, light always wins.

Light always reveals. Light always heals.

The darkness that creeps in the hidden corners of your heart fears being revealed, for it does not understand the healing power my light brings.

Invite my light to take root in your life. Fall into the warmth of my light; you will find healing there. As you breathe, feel my life rush through your lungs giving life to your entire body. As you wake, know the light of my salvation upon you and walk in it.

Reading
2

What do you hear?

LIVE

How will you respond?

A prompt for living

Write a card to a friend or co-worker to speak life over them. What do you see as their gifts? What do you feel is a way you have witnessed them bring good to those around them? Write it in a card and share it!

LISTEN
John 1:6-8

⁶ *There was a man sent from God whose name was John.* ⁷ *He came as a witness to testify concerning that light, so that through him all might believe.* ⁸ *He himself was not the light; he came only as a witness to the light.*

I have sent loved ones into the world to bear witness of my work. They are great story tellers, artists, speakers, friends, business men and women, truck drivers, teachers, directors, producers, musicians, moms, dads, students, and even toddlers. I have sent those I love to bear witness.

You have had one of my witnesses speak to you. You've heard, seen, or experienced my life-giving truth through another. They have invited you to my light; to me.

I have also given you a task.

What do you hear?

Reading 3

As you follow me, you are also to bear witness to what I have done in your life.

As you follow me, you are to use your place to speak of my truth.

As you follow me, I will make you radiant and you will shine. You will shine to a world in desperate need of my light.

LIVE

Think now of your friends, co-workers, neighbors, and relatives. Think of the stranger, the alien, the orphan. Think of those in your life, those around the world who have not witnessed my light.

O loved one, shine. Shine my light to the watching world. As you shine, entrust the fruit of your task to my care.

Be a witness to my light and shine for all the world to see.

How will you respond?

A prompt for living

Today, take a moment to tell a story of the goodness of God in your life with someone. Take time to ask that person how they have experienced His goodness in the last week. Celebrate together in some way.

LISTEN
John 1:9-13

9 The true light that gives light to everyone was coming into the world. 10 He was in the world, and though the world was made through him, the world did not recognize him. 11 He came to that which was his own, but his own did not receive him. 12 Yet to all who did receive him, to those who believed in his name, he gave the right to become children of God- 13 children born not of natural descent, nor of human decision or a husband's will, but born of God.

I am your Father. I am your loving, caring, attentive, and gracious Father. I have adopted you into my family. I have chosen you.

I know your exact condition and I have chosen you to be a part of my family.

From the very beginning of time I have chosen people to bear my image and my likeness. I made Adam and Eve in my likeness and it was very good. They chose to ignore my image in them and the truth of my character and love for them, to turn to a lie. The lie seemed much more believable. I grieved as I watched them choose death over life.

Now every person has the same invitation before them. I have invited you to be a part of my family. I've put my image on you and like a natural father, I want you to carry my name and share in my inheritance.

I long for you to walk in the truth of my name and the power of belonging to my kingdom family.

Dear child, choose to believe, work to believe, not just for an instant but, in all things. Trust my voice and my love for you.

I am a loving Father, not won over by accomplishment, but simply love because you are my child.

Believe in this love. Live out of this grace. You are my child, I adopted you into my family just as you are, and it is good.

What do you hear?

LIVE

How will you respond?

A prompt for living

As a member of the family of God, you have the authority to bless others in His name and in His power. Who do you want to bless today? Pray blessing over every business you walk into, person with whom you interact, and place your feet stand.

LISTEN

John 1:14

14 The Word became flesh and made his dwelling among us. We have seen his glory, the glory of the one and only Son, who came from the Father, full of grace and truth.

The very Word that spoke life into existence came to you. My son; He took on flesh and entered the very world he created. My son; full of life, full of truth, embracing my every way, came.

He came for you.

My love for you is deep and it is full of grace and truth.

I long for you to know this grace. It is a grace that meets you in your inadequacy and brokenness and pours life over you and pours love into your veins. I long for you to know truth. To know truth that speaks life into your soul and transforms the way you think about yourself and others. My grace and truth are a perfect gift and they come wrapped in sacrifice and love.

I long for you to walk in these realities every moment of every day. I long for you to know this Word, my very Son; who by definition is life.

I know that you struggle to believe. I know that you doubt. I know that logic is your companion and human logic goes against the way of my kingdom. I know that you want answers. Come to me for those answers. Ask me. Don't be afraid of that which you cannot understand; grace and truth, love and sacrifice do not come naturally in a world that drives hard against them. If you ask me, I will show you. I have given you the very word of life in my Son and this word I will show you as you seek my face.

I love you. I love you with an everlasting love. I love you with a life-changing love. I love you forever and always.

Walk in the way of the Word, my Son, full of grace and truth.

READING

5

What do you hear?

LIVE

How will you respond?

A prompt for living

When tempted to withhold grace and good, offer it freely. Give generously to someone who does not deserve it.

LISTEN
John 1:15-18

15 (John testified concerning him. He cried out, saying, "This is the one I spoke about when I said, 'He who comes after me has surpassed me because he was before me.'")

16 Out of his fullness we have all received grace in place of grace already given.

17 For the law was given through Moses; grace and truth came through Jesus Christ.

18 No one has ever seen God, but the one and only Son, who is himself God and [b] is in closest relationship with the Father, has made him known.

When you wonder where I am, look to Jesus. When you wonder what I've done, look to Jesus. When you are looking for a way, look to Jesus.

I sent my Son, who is himself God, to show you me. He is the very picture of me. He came to embody grace and truth, expressed through love and sacrifice. He is my very likeness. He is my gift to you.

When you wonder how you'll get out of your situation, look to Jesus.

When you wonder if you're alone, cling to Jesus.

When you wonder, doubt or fear, look to Jesus.

Yes, as you live in this world you will have trouble, and when you do, look to Jesus—you'll find me. You'll see my love expressed, my hope given, my grace lavished, and my truth revealed.

Look to Jesus.

You'll find me.

What do you hear?

LIVE

How will you respond?

A prompt for living

Do you have a friend who is hurting? Or a co-worker in a tough spot? Maybe it is a class mate of yours or your child or their parents? Take a moment to take inventory of the people with whom you interact and note where they may be experiencing hurt or disappointment. Make a point to offer encouragement, show a small kindness, offer help where needed, or do something small to communicate to the person that they are seen and that they are not alone.

LISTEN
John 1:19-20

[19] Now this was John's testimony when the Jewish leaders[c] in Jerusalem sent priests and Levites to ask him who he was. [20] He did not fail to confess, but confessed freely, "I am not the Messiah."

You carry the weight of other's choices on your shoulders. You seek to understand and help bring life and freedom to those with whom you come in contact. Your heart longs for others to know Jesus, but you get confused along the way.

It is not yours to save. It is mine to save.

It is not yours to heal. It is mine to heal.

It is not yours to free. It is mine to free.

It is not yours to restore. It is mine to restore.

You are not salvation, but you are a conduit for my salvation.

You are not the healer. You are a conduit for my healing.

You are not the giver of freedom. You are a conduit of my freedom.

It is important that you know who you are and who I am. For when you seek to live out a mission that is not yours to take on, you will find only trappings of pride, discouragement, addiction to work, and need for approval. When you live out of your created way as a conduit for my salvation, healing, freedom, and restoration, you yourself experience them first.

Trust in my work. Believe in my name. And step into your role as my ambassador, a conduit for my good in the world.

What do you hear?

LIVE

How will you respond?

A prompt for living

Go to a spot you frequent: coffee shop, grocery store, work place, church, or anywhere else where you have built a relationship with those on staff. Bring a thank you note and a small gift to show your appreciation to those who work there. Speak to how they have been a conduit of good in your life.

LISTEN
John 1:21-23

21 They asked him, "Then who are you? Are you Elijah?"
He said, "I am not."
"Are you the Prophet?"
He answered, "No."

22 Finally they said, "Who are you? Give us an answer to take back to those who sent us. What do you say about yourself?"

23 John replied in the words of Isaiah the prophet, "I am the voice of one calling in the wilderness, 'Make straight the way for the Lord.'" [d]

I have given you a voice, and I've given you a message.

It is yours to speak and your unique voice will deliver it in a way only you can.

I have created you with great intention and purpose. I have called you out of the wilderness to speak my name among those in your life's path.

Often you struggle to think that your voice, and your audience is not enough. This is a lie.

I have created you for a specific purpose. I have created you with a particular audience in mind. Trust this.

You are enough.

You have what it takes.

I've given you place and purpose.

I've set a message in your heart and it is good.

I am the author of your message and I am the one who has given you a voice. I set you in the midst of those who will listen to your voice. Lean into this truth and speak.

What do you hear?

LIVE

How will you respond?

A prompt for living

Use your voice today to speak life over those with whom you come in contact. And, when an opportunity for conversation presents itself, offer your story of God's good in your life.

LISTEN
John 1:24-28

24 Now the Pharisees who had been sent 25 questioned him, "Why then do you baptize if you are not the Messiah, nor Elijah, nor the Prophet?"

26 "I baptize with [e] water," John replied, "but among you stands one you do not know. 27 He is the one who comes after me, the straps of whose sandals I am not worthy to untie." 28 This all happened at Bethany on the other side of the Jordan, where John was baptizing.

I have placed people throughout the ages, spanning the nations to speak of me. I have put them in positions to speak of me among those who do not know me.

Many will not recognize me. It is yours to point me out to the world in which you live.

My child, I have shown you my name and unveiled my character to you. I have given you a glimpse of my kingdom and have allowed you to share in it.

You will come against those who do not yet know my name.

You will have those in your life who speak against me. Those who doubt will cross your path. Pay attention! I am doing something good and none of this is by accident. I have given you authority to speak of me among those who are saved and those who are perishing.

Look for opportunities to serve, to teach, to give, and to answer. I will give you what you need in the moment; do not be afraid. I've not placed you in your community or put a burden on your heart for which I've not already equipped you.

READING

9

What do you hear?

LIVE

How will you respond?

A prompt for living

When you see good, speak it. When you experience beauty, speak it. When you are provided for, speak it. When you experience the goodness of God in any way, tell the story. Tell the story not as one trying to convince another, but simply to speak of what is true in your story. Speak of Jesus as if He is a person with whom you engage daily, as you would speak of a friend or family member. Tell of His wonderful acts!

LISTEN
John 1:29-31

29 The next day John saw Jesus coming toward him and said, "Look, the Lamb of God, who takes away the sin of the world! 30 This is the one I meant when I said, 'A man who comes after me has surpassed me because he was before me.' 31 I myself did not know him, but the reason I came baptizing with water was that he might be revealed to Israel."

I have come. I am among you. I am for you. I have come to remove from you all that seeks to kill, steal, and destroy. The enemy runs around seeking to devour and so often you believe his words over mine. They affirm in you a belief that you are not enough and that you are unacceptable. This grieves me.

The sin which so easily entangles you keeps you distant. It also keeps you from seeing what is true. When you believe lies about yourself and others my truth sounds foolish. You are lovely, seen, special, created, set apart, loved, beloved, and mine. I accept you and want you to live in the power of my acceptance. This is life.

That which keeps you from walking in this truth is sin, the lies of the enemy lived out as truth. Die to these lies and live new in me.

I have come to bring you life. I have come to speak life into and over you. I have come that you might make agreement with me. Yes, I am the great sacrifice. I, the Lamb of God, the sacrifice, have come to unite you with life and to and keep you into relationship with me.

READING
10

What do you hear?

LIVE

How will you respond?

A prompt for living

Think of a friend or family member who is struggling to believe good about him or herself. Seek them out and speak the good you see in them.

Or, take a moment to highlight a company you love on your social media outlet. Tell of an experience you have with them and share the good they are doing. The public praise will encourage in ways that might surprise you!

LISTEN
John 1:32-34

32 Then John gave this testimony: "I saw the Spirit come down from heaven as a dove and remain on him. 33 And I myself did not know him, but the one who sent me to baptize with water told me, 'The man on whom you see the Spirit come down and remain is the one who will baptize with the Holy Spirit.' 34 I have seen and I testify that this is God's Chosen One." [f]

I know that at times you doubt.

Hold on to my word.

I know at times you question.

Hold on to my promise.

I know at times you cannot see.

Ask me to reveal myself to you.

I know at times you do not hear.

Ask to hear my voice.

I know at times you do not believe.

Ask for me to show you things of my kingdom.

I know that the work of belief is hard. I know that belief is process. I know that you want to believe and at times it feels as though you've become blind and deaf to me. When you hit these times and you experience these seasons, trust me and choose to believe.

I will make myself known to all who seek me.

Seek me with all of your heart, I will be found.

Knock, I will open the door.

Ask, I will answer.

Trust, and your life will know my everlasting life.

You will know life through Jesus, my chosen one.

I love you dear child. I will not leave you in the dark, nor will I abandon you in your time of trouble. In this world you will have trouble, doubt, fear, and experience periods where you do not recognize that I'm with you. But take heart! I, I have overcome the world.

What do you hear?

LIVE

How will you respond?

A prompt for living

Choose a name or character trait of God. Invite a friend to look for that name or trait throughout your days and share your lists with each other weekly. Commit to one month of looking and seeing together.

LISTEN
John 1:35-37

35 The next day John was there again with two of his disciples. 36 When he saw Jesus passing by, he said, "Look, the Lamb of God!" 37 When the two disciples heard him say this, they followed Jesus.

You bear witness to me. You speak of me with your words and you speak of me with your actions.

There are many who do not know me. There are many who are not yet able to put a face to the One pursuing them. There are those who have only been shown a religious version of me and have turned away from me in response.

My child, it is my desire that you would recognize me and that you would point others to me.

My hope is, that not only will you be a light, but that you'd be a conduit for others to connect with me.

I desire to reveal myself through the way you live.

I desire to reveal myself through your words.

I desire to reveal myself through your work, dreams, and visions.

I desire for you, my child, to point others to me.

When you see evidence of me, say so.

It is my desire that all will know my name and follow me. For I am life and I want every person, everywhere, to connect to my life and my light.

READING
12

What do you hear?

LIVE

How will you respond?

A prompt for living

Go on a hunt in your workplace for evidence of good in those around you. For each person you see engage in good and for each act of goodness by the company speak it and thank them for how they are adding good to the world and your workplace.

LISTEN
John 1:38-39

38 Turning around, Jesus saw them following and asked, "What do you want?" They said, "Rabbi" (which means "Teacher"), "where are you staying?"
39 "Come," he replied, "and you will see." So they went and saw where he was staying, and they spent that day with him. It was about four in the afternoon.

I want to know what you want. It's a question that I ask of you and much of the time you are afraid to answer. You respond with phrases like, "I want what you want," or "I want what will make you happy."

What you want is important to me. What you want gives a window into your soul. It gives a picture of your most vulnerable places and your deepest places of desire, longing, fulfillment, and discouragement.

I mean it when I ask you what you want.

So let me ask you again, "What do you want my child?"

As you come to know what you want, you also come to trust with deeper dependence. You come to cling to me for the response or the fulfillment of a desire. Your wants lead to dependence on me.

I love to answer people. I love for my children to know that I am with them, I am for them, and I care.

I want my children to know that their Father will withhold no good thing.

Trust me when you want.

Trust that I mean it when I ask.

Trust that I am good and desire good for you.

I love you dearly.

What do you hear?

LIVE

How will you respond?

A prompt for living

Is there a want in you that has not been met? There are wants in many around you that are also not met. Take time today to pray for those around you who have unfulfilled desires. Pray that they will have hope. If it feel appropriate, let the person know that you are praying for them in this area.

LISTEN
John 1:40-42

⁴⁰ Andrew, Simon Peter's brother, was one of the two who heard what John had said and who had followed Jesus. ⁴¹ The first thing Andrew did was to find his brother Simon and tell him, "We have found the Messiah" (that is, the Christ). ⁴² And he brought him to Jesus. Jesus looked at him and said, "You are Simon son of John. You will be called Cephas" (which, when translated, is Peter[g]).

I have given you a new name.

When you come to me, I take you as I find you and I give you a vision of what could be and what will be when you place your faith in me.

You come to me unknown and I will make you known.

You come to me weak and I will make you strong.

You've been given the name of unacceptable and I have changed it to chosen and acceptable.

You've been given the name ugly and I tell you your name is beautiful.

You've been given the name stupid and I give you the name wise.

You've been given the name selfish and I call you generous.

I have changed your name, just as I did with my servant Peter, I now do for you. I have called you from obscurity and normalcy, and I have given you the name of child of God, set apart, glorious, capable, and loved.

Your new name is an accurate reflection of the way things are. Your new name is not a pipe dream. I don't believe in pipe dreams.

I called Simon, Peter, the rock. And I did build my church on him.

I do not give false names.

Come to me, come and see what I have for you. Come and learn how I see you. Come, come to me, and receive your new name.

What do you hear?

LIVE

How will you respond?

A prompt for living

Pay attention when people call themselves various names around you. When they speak of a name that is not filled with life, remind them of who they really are! Hold the person accountable to the good image in which they were designed.

LISTEN
John 1:43

43 The next day Jesus decided to leave for Galilee. Finding Philip, he said to him, "Follow me."

Sweet child, you are not a child any longer. I have given you the name capable and acceptable and I see you as an adult. As an adult, I ask you to do one thing.

I ask you to follow me.

I know that you do not follow anything in which you do not believe. Therefore, I know I'm asking more of you than a game of follow the leader in your back yard.

I am asking you to listen to me, believe my words, and follow me wherever I take you.

I will take you to many unexpected places. Some you will find comforting, some exciting, some uncomfortable, so out right illogical.

I am asking you to follow, not lead, not even explore on your own, but follow.

This means I will go before you.

I will never lead you to a place where I've not stepped before you.

I will never ask you to follow me only to abandon you.

I ask you to follow because I only lead people to life. This is difficult for you to understand, because the idea of life you've been given is tainted and often is not life at all.

I am the life and only lead you to life. As you follow me, you too will know life and it shall be good.

Follow me.

READING

15

What do you hear?

LIVE

How will you respond?

A prompt for living

Do you know someone who is lost? Who does not know what direction to choose? Take a moment to call, text, or write an email or a card to let them know that you are praying with them as they seek where to go and who to follow.

LISTEN
John 1:44-46

⁴⁴ Philip, like Andrew and Peter, was from the town of Bethsaida. ⁴⁵ Philip found Nathanael and told him, "We have found the one Moses wrote about in the Law, and about whom the prophets also wrote-Jesus of Nazareth, the son of Joseph."
⁴⁶ "Nazareth! Can anything good come from there?" Nathanael asked. "Come and see," said Philip.

Come and see. I am doing the unexpected among you. I am showing myself to people around the world. Come and see.

I am creating beauty every day. Come and see.

I am bringing peace amidst conflict. Come and see.

I am showing up in significant ways in the lives of individuals. Come and see.

I am using my bride, the church, to do marvelous things. Come and see.

I am constantly inviting you to sight.

I am continually showing myself to you.

I show and it is yours to tell.

I am showing myself to people around the world. Go and tell.

I am creating beauty every day. Go and tell.

I am bringing peace amidst conflict. Go and tell.

I am showing up in significant ways in the lives of individuals. Go and tell.

I am using my bride, the church, to do marvelous things. Go and tell.

I am inviting you to participate in the world's most important game of show and tell.

Watch and speak. Watch for me every day. And, tell of my marvelous acts. Tell the stories of my healing among the nations.

Yes, I am at work and often it comes in unexpected ways.

Look and invite others to sight!

What do you hear?

LIVE

How will you respond?

A prompt for living

1. **Practice seeing.** Make a list today of all the ways which you saw God at work. This takes training. Remember God's names and attributes: beauty, peace, grace, good, friend, healer, love, joy, light, and more. When you don't know how to look for God, remember his names and attributes to guide your sight.

2. **Practice telling.** Tell the story of good, beauty, grace, healing, hope, etc. to someone in your life once today.

47 When Jesus saw Nathanael approaching, he said of him, "Here truly is an Israelite in whom there is no deceit."
48 "How do you know me?" Nathanael asked. Jesus answered, "I saw you while you were still under the fig tree before Philip called you."
49 Then Nathanael declared, "Rabbi, you are the Son of God; you are the king of Israel."
50 Jesus said, "You believe because I told you I saw you under the fig tree. You will see greater things than that." 51 He then added, "Very truly I tell you, you will see 'heaven open, and the angels of God ascending and descending on' the Son of Man."

I know you long to be known. I know that you want to be seen. It is not a surprise to me that you want to be heard. When I created man and woman, I did so with purpose. I put inside of you a desire to be known, to be seen, and to be heard.

When Adam and Eve chose to believe a lie and made an agreement with the enemy, they began hiding. They no longer wanted to be seen. This went against my created design. There is freedom in truth and one who is fully seen, is known and is free. Truth always will lead to relationship with me.

I long for you to believe me and to trust me with your life; to trust that I see you and know you and love you. To trust that I want to hear you and listen to what is on your heart and in your mind. There is a great lie the enemy feeds you, it is the thought that I will not love you if I see or know you or hear truth from you. This devastates me. O, my child, believe in my sight and love. Believe that they are compassionate and that I am a God who is kind. Believe me in this. My child, trust that I, the God who sees, is also Love by very definition.

I do see you. I do know you. I do hear you.

Believe.

What do you hear?

LIVE

How will you respond?

A prompt for living

Practice seeing and loving: Today take a moment to think about a friend, co-worker, neighbor or relative who hides in some way.

As a name comes to mind, make a point to encourage that person this week in some way. Let him/her know that you see them and that you love them.

John 2 (Readings 18–23)

LISTEN
John 2:1-4

Reading

18

¹ On the third day a wedding took place at Cana in Galilee. Jesus' mother was there, ² and Jesus and his disciples had also been invited to the wedding. ³ When the wine was gone, Jesus' mother said to him, "They have no more wine."
⁴ "Woman, why do you involve me?" Jesus replied. "My hour has yet come."

I know you desire to know my plan.

I know that there are prayers you've prayed that I've seemingly not answered.

I know you cry out for another's salvation.

I am intimately aware that you have a need that must be met.

I also know the needs of every person in your life's path.

I know that you long for their needs to be met.

I truly understand that there are desires you have that are yet to be fulfilled.

I know the cares you carry.

I know the tears you cry, the fears to which you cling, and the unanswered questions that you still hold.

I know.

I care.

I am not ignoring you.

I am not cold-hearted or without compassion.

There is great purpose in every single act of my hand.

And—my timing is perfect.

I reveal answers, meet needs, grant desires, awaken hearts, bring salvation, and release burdens within perfect timing. I know details your eyes do not see, and I will not reveal myself early.

I know when one is ripe, having the deepest level of receptivity to me and my way.

Trust me in this.

Continue to ask. Bring every desire to me. I AM—your great provider.

What do you hear?

LIVE

How will you respond?

A prompt for living

Today take some time to pray for one person in your life, then let them know. Write a card, a Facebook message, tweet them, email them, call them, or text them. The form does not matter. Simply letting them know that you remembered them and went to the Lord on their behalf will be a great encouragement!

LISTEN
John 2:5-10

⁵ His mother said to the servants, "Do whatever he tells you." ⁶ Nearby stood six stone water jars, the kind used by the Jews for ceremonial washing, each holding from twenty to thirty gallons. ⁷ Jesus said to the servants, "Fill the jars with water"; so they filled them to the brim. ⁸ Then he told them, "Now draw some out and take it to the master of the banquet." They did so, ⁹ and the master of the banquet tasted the water that had been turned into wine. He did not realize where it had come from, though the servants who had drawn the water knew. Then he called the bridegroom aside ¹⁰ and said, "Everyone brings out the choice wine first and then the cheaper wine after the guests have had too much to drink; but you have saved the best till now."

Today I bring you good things; things that come in all sorts of packages. Have you seen them?

The things I bring are beautiful, wonderful, and rich.

Often you see what I bring and you credit me. I can also come undercover.

Unless you pay close attention you may miss my blessings all together.

People are often given credit for my miracles. You have been credited for work I've done.

I use you for miraculous things without your knowledge.

I love to surprise my children with good. I am delighted when the best comes at the most unexpected time.

I have given you great good. Take a moment to think back on your day; was there anything good in it? Were you aware of the ways I blessed, protected, or surprised you with good? Ask me, I will show you. Were you aware when I used you today?

Was there good I asked of you? Did you respond to the nudge with a yes?

Often you think you're filling up a jar with water, and I have much grander plans. I take your obedience and expand it to bless others, speak about my kingdom, and reveal myself.

Look around, pay attention and respond. Good is a part of your life. It's so good you can taste it!

What do you hear?

LIVE

How will you respond?

A prompt for living

Today make a list of the good things you experience.

Make another list of the times you felt prompted in some way to remember, encourage, give to, hug, smile at, speak kindly to, offer your time, serve in some way, or simply respect someone. Thank the Lord for giving good to you and through you!

LISTEN
John 2:11

11 What Jesus did here in Cana of Galilee was the first of the signs through which he revealed his glory; and his disciples believed in him.

I am full of many wonders. I fill the sky with stars that radiantly shine. I raise mountains high above the valleys. The trees sway with the wind, the sky blue and brilliant. I've laid out a canvas of beauty and majesty for all to see. My creation tells my story and speaks to my glory.

You have experienced miraculous things.

You have been transformed.

You continue to be transformed.

You've known provision, help, hope, healing, grace, love, friendship, and blessing in the nick of time. In my right time.

You've experienced pain. You've been stripped of that which holds you down. You have known suffering and loss and you've tasted darkness and this darkness has not overcome you. I have held you through the pain, the loss, the suffering, and I've given you enough light to make it through each day.

My glory comes in many packages. It is full of grace and truth. It is full of wonder and beauty.

My glory is unfathomable.

My glory will come to you. It has come to you.

My glory raises you out of the pit, sustains you in the valley, sings through creation, shouts from the tops of mountains and gently soothes you as the wind gently brushes your face.

I am full of many wonders and my glory is for you to see.

What do you hear?

LIVE

How will you respond?

A prompt for living

Today take note of creation. What does it teach you about the glory of God?

Tell a story to a friend about the glory of God revealed in a season of your life.

LISTEN
John 2:13-17

13 When it was almost time for the Jewish Passover, Jesus went up to Jerusalem. 14 In the temple courts he found people selling cattle, sheep and doves, and others sitting at tables exchanging money. 15 So he made a whip out of cords, and drove all from the temple courts, both sheep and cattle; he scattered the coins of the money changers and overturned their tables. 16 To those who sold doves he said, "Get these out of here! Stop turning my Father's house into a market!" 17 His disciples remembered that it is written: "Zeal for your house will consume me."

I have zeal for my church today. I have placed in you a zeal for my name. I have also placed you in a body, a house, of millions of others who follow me, called my church.

My church will be a house of prayer, a house of worship, a house of friendship, a house of justice, a house of righteousness, a house of mercy, and a house of love.

My house, my body, my church bring me honor when those who inhabit it live out these qualities in their lives together and alone.

I despise when my house is used to speak any other message.

What do you hear?

LIVE

How will you respond?

A prompt for living

Briefly write out what message you exhibit with your life.

Write what message you want to exhibit.

Make one conscious choice to exhibit love, mercy, or justice to someone today.

LISTEN
John 2:18-22

18 The Jews then responded to him, "What sign can you show us to prove your authority to do all this?"
19 Jesus answered them, "Destroy this temple, and I will raise it again in three days."
20 They replied, "It has taken forty-six years to build this temple, and you are going to raise it in three days?" 21 But the temple he had spoken of was his body. 22 After he was raised from the dead, his disciples recalled what he had said. Then they believed the scripture and the words that Jesus had spoken.

I am always ahead of you.

I put people in your life today for events that have not yet come.

I have had words spoken over you today that will one day come to bear witness to me or encourage you in a time of need.

I have given you provision today for times ahead.

I have given you ideas today, for problems that will arise in years down the road.

I live in your past, present, and future. I speak out of and into each space of time all of the time.

Your eyes can only see what is behind you and right in front of you, they cannot see five years or even five minutes ahead.

When a person comes into your life, treasure them and know that they've been given as a gift for such a time as this.

When a word of encouragement is spoken over you that doesn't make sense, hold on to it, it will one day.

I create in you a vault of experiences, people, encouragements, and resources for your time of trial.

One day, you too will remember these words and I will be glorified.

READING
22

What do you hear?

LIVE

How will you respond?

A prompt for living

Ask Jesus to speak to you the name of a friend, co-worker, family member, neighbor, or acquaintance. Write down the name that comes to mind.

Pray that God will show you how to encourage that person this week and then put that idea into motion!

LISTEN
John 2:23-25

23 Now while he was in Jerusalem at the Passover Festival, many people saw the signs he was performing and believed in his name. 24 But Jesus would not entrust himself to them, for he knew all people. 25 He did not need any testimony about mankind, for he knew what was in each person.

You study, labor, and strain to know much about me. You read books, listen to sermons, learn from intellectuals and great minds, and you have come to know many facts and ideas about who I am.

I know you. I know what is in your mind.

I know what is in your heart. I see your every way.

I am intimately familiar with your deepest fears, greatest accomplishments, and places of inadequacies.

I know you; for I created you.

I created your mind to be curious. I created your heart to feel.

I created your body to sense. I created your spirit to raise awareness.

I know you.

I know you intimately.

Knowing does not come as an exercise of the mind. It is a comprehensive act of your whole self.

For you to know me, you must sit with me, recognize me, hear me, be familiar with my scent, know my touch, and feel my presence. I am he who created your senses and each of them was given to you so that you would be able to know me and believe.

What do you hear?

LIVE

How will you respond?

A prompt for living

Make of the list of the things you know about your best friend.

Do the same thing with Jesus. Make a list of the things you know about him.

Choose one character trait about Jesus to look for throughout your day and share your list with a friend to encourage them at day's end.

JOHN 3   (Readings 24–33)

LISTEN
John 3:1-2

¹ Now there was a Pharisee, a man named Nicodemus who was a member of the Jewish ruling council. ² He came to Jesus at night and said, "Rabbi, we know that you are a teacher who has come from God. For no one could perform the signs you are doing if God were not with him."

Your life is the proof of where your identity lies.

Your life gives the evidence of your belief.

Your life bears fruit that shows off your root system.

When your roots are in me, your life will bear the fruit of love, joy, peace, patience, kindness, goodness, gentleness, and self-control.

When your roots are in me, you will always be ready to give an answer for the hope that is within you, for hope will be in you.

When your roots are in me, you will act justly, love mercy, and walk humbly.

When your roots are in me, you will care for the widow and orphan.

When your roots are in me, you will love your enemy and pray for those who persecute you.

When your roots are in me, you will know a peace that surpasses all understanding.

When your roots are in me, you will have a gentle and quite spirit.

When your roots are in me, you will know truth and you will be free.

The fruit of your life is the evidence of your root system and your root system is the very source of your identity.

My child, you are a member of my family, a royal priesthood, a holy nation, a people belonging to God.

May your life bear fruit of this fact.

What do you hear?

LIVE

How will you respond?

A prompt for living

Choose one person in your life who exudes Jesus and write them an email, post card, letter, tweet or whatever, and tell them that their life bears fruit that points you to Jesus.

LISTEN
John 3:3-8

³ Jesus replied, "Very truly I tell you, no one can see the kingdom of God unless they are born again."
⁴ "How can someone be born when they are old?" Nicodemus asked. "Surely they cannot enter a second time into their mother's womb to be born!"
⁵ Jesus answered, "Very truly I tell you, no one can enter the kingdom of God unless they are born of water and the Spirit. ⁶ Flesh gives birth to flesh, but the Spirit gives birth to spirit. ⁷ You should not be surprised at my saying, 'You must be born again.' ⁸ The wind blows wherever it pleases. You hear its sound, but you cannot tell where it comes from or where it is going. So it is with everyone born of the Spirit."

I give life to all things. I give life to body and spirit. When you are born, your body and mind come to life. Your spirit awaits a meeting with me.

I long for every spirit to awaken to my way and to have life and have it to the fullest.

Full life comes as each part of your whole self collides with my life giving way.

You look to many things to give you life. You look to success.

You look to a healthy body. You look to comfort, popularity, security, and safety.

You look to many things to bring you life that actually bring the contrary.

Life does not come from temporary things; it comes from only one source and that is Me.

Trust in this. Believe this. Come to Me and receive life that is true and everlasting.

What do you hear?

LIVE

How will you respond?

A prompt for living

Think of one person in your life who does not know Jesus. Ask Jesus to speak to you life-giving words for him/her.

When you have words to say, share those in some way with that friend. Write a card, meet them for a beer, take a walk, or call them up. Do whatever you must to connect with them, and share with them words of life.

9 "How can this be?" Nicodemus asked.
10 "You are Israel's teacher," said Jesus, "and do you not understand these things? 11 Very truly I tell you, we speak of what we know, and we testify to what we have seen, but still you people do not accept our testimony. 12 I have spoken to you of earthly things and you do not believe; how then will you believe if I speak of heavenly things? 13 No one has ever gone into heaven except the one who came from heaven the Son of Man. 14 Just as Moses lifted up the snake in the wilderness, so the Son of Man must be lifted up, 15 that everyone who believes may have eternal life in him."

As you trust in me, you trust in the things of heaven. The things of heaven are vastly different from the things of earth. The things of earth head in the opposite direction of my care, my love, and my way.

Because of this, my ways seem unnatural to you. My ways feel unknown and uncomfortable.

I have come to rescue. I have come save.

I have come to bring a way of life.

I have come from heaven to bring a new way.

I have come to bring eternal life and an eternal way.

As you walk through life, trust that my way is good and my law is love.

I have not come to kill, steal, or destroy. I know at times this is what you believe. This is a lie.

My dear child, come to me with your questions. Come to me with your doubts. Come to me when you're hurting. Come to me when you're confused. Come to me and I will bring to you the greatest gift; the gift of everlasting life.

Breathe in this truth. It is good and it is for you.

I will open your eyes to it, so look to me, look for me and believe.

I love you dearly my child.

What do you hear?

LIVE

How will you respond?

A prompt for living

For what does your heart break?

Write your answer in your journal or make a note on your computer.

Bring your answer to the Lord and ask him what the way of heaven says about it.

Adopt one practice to your weekly rhythm that breathes life into that which breaks your heart. That may come in a variety of packages, letters, lobbying, monetary donations, time volunteered, or raising awareness with those who do not know. Bring the way of heaven to that which breaks your heart!

LISTEN
John 3:16

16 For God so loved the world that he gave his one and only Son, that whoever believes in him shall not perish but have eternal life.

My love is not limited. My love does not come with circumstances and conditions attached to it. In love I created the entire earth and in love I created you. My love is deep and high and wide and long. My love is greater than any human understanding.

My love is full of sacrifice. My love is full of generosity.

My love is complete. My love is abundant. My love is full. My love is for the world. My love gives joy. My love gives hope.

My love gave you breath and my love takes your breath away.

In love I sent my love, my Son, to earth. In love I gave my Son to you, so that when you see him and you believe in him, you would see my love; like light in darkness and you would believe. When you believe in my Son, you receive my love and you live in his love—which, is my love.

I gave my one and only Son, to you, my love, so that you could live in my eternal love. This is what true love is, when one gives their life for another. I am that love. I am your love.

What do you hear?

LIVE

How will you respond?

A prompt for living

Who do you love?

Is there a part of the world, a neighbor, a friend, a celebrity, a politician, a co-worker a neighborhood for which you have a unique love?

Today, pray for that which you love. Pray that they will be transformed by the love of God.

Do something to communicate love sacrificially for this person, people group, or place.

Go and clean up the neighborhood, write a letter to the president, tweet a prayer to a celebrity, buy a co-worker lunch, bake cookies for your neighbor. In some way . . . show love as you pray they'd come to know love!

LISTEN
John 3:17

17 For God did not send his Son into the world to condemn the world, but to save the world through him.

I do not delight in condemnation. I did not send my Son to you to condemn you. My intent was to save. My intent is always salvation.

You get caught up in condemnation. It overcomes your mind and heart and you wear it like an anvil around your neck.
You focus much of your attention on what you've done that is against my will or where you feel you don't measure up. You seem to revel in your sin nature, boasting that you are nothing but a sinful creature. You bring this condemnation to me thinking that it will make me glad that you've finally seen the truth!

This attitude is not from me. I have come to bring you salvation. I have come to bring you love. I have come to bring you an inheritance. I have come to change your name.

There is therefore, now no condemnation for those who are in my Son.

I sent my Son to bring salvation, hope, healing, restoration, and love. Let this be your focus.

Live into the reality and grace of my salvation.

Let the burden of condemnation fall from your shoulders and be lifted up.

I've rescued you from the pit, out of the mud and mire and I have set you on a rock. Do not think about the mire and the pit from which you were rescued, instead turn your attention to the rock on which you now stand; the grace and salvation that I sent my Son to offer.

What do you hear?

LIVE

How will you respond?

A prompt for living

What is an issue that really gets you going?

Something that makes you angry. . . .

Take time to pray for those who participate in or agree with that which makes you mad.

Ask that God will reveal his saving grace to them and that he would allow you to build a relationship with someone who supports that which you despise.

Come up with a practical way you can love and speak God's saving grace over this person or those people. And do it!

LISTEN
John 3:18

18 Whoever believes in him is not condemned, but whoever does not believe stands condemned already because they have not believed in the name of God's one and only Son.

My son is essential.	He is I AM.	He is My Son.	He is Immanuel.
My son is the way.	He is Beloved.	He is Lord.	He is the Lamb who was slain.
He is the truth.	He is Salvation.	He is Prince of Peace.	
He is the life.	He is Freedom.	He is Creator.	He was.
He is the Word.	He is Son of Man.	He is Teacher.	He is. He forever shall be.

My son, Jesus, was given the name that is above *every* name.
That at the name of *Jesus*, every knee will bow and tongue confess, that HE is Lord. To my glory!

Believe in His name.

READING
29

What do you hear?

LIVE

How will you respond?

A prompt for living

Who do you condemn?

Confess this condemnation, and pray for this person or people group to believe.

Go out of your way to show kindness to this person or people group this week. Remembering, it is the kindness of the Lord that leads to repentance!

LISTEN
John 3:19-21

19 This is the verdict: Light has come into the world, but people loved darkness instead of light because their deeds were evil. 20 Everyone who does evil hates the light, and will not come into the light for fear that their deeds will be exposed. 21 But whoever lives by the truth comes into the light, so that it may be seen plainly that what they have done has been done in the sight of God.

At times you love the darkness. You cower into a dark room or corner and stay there with hopes that you will not be found out.

Shame and guilt keep you in the darkness. Fear overwhelms you there. Captivity is the experience of the darkness.

You condemn yourself to stay in the dark and you stay there for fear that you'd be exposed for what truly is. The darkness is filled with lies, heaviness, and burdens.

It is in the darkness that you avoid the healing warmth of my light.

I invite you to light. I invite you to be exposed. I invite you to come out of hiding. Light reveals the truth and living in the truth is living in freedom.

Fear of light is evidence that you do not fully embrace my love and believe the words I have told you. My love is not contingent upon your behavior. My love is freely given. My love does not come with condition or a scale of approval.

It is my desire that you live in the light, truth, and freedom that I offer. I will constantly invite you to live in such a way, for when you live in light you embrace my love and grace. Receive my love, be met by my grace and live in the light.

What do you hear?

LIVE

How will you respond?

A prompt for living

Do you know someone in hiding?

Ask God to reveal to you a person who is living in darkness or shame.

Do something today to love them without condition. Write a card for no reason. Ask them to coffee. Invite them to your home for dinner.

Invite Jesus to use you as a conduit of love and light in their life and actively pursue a relationship of light with them!

LISTEN
John 3:22-30

²² After this, Jesus and his disciples went out into the Judean countryside, where he spent some time with them, and baptized. ²³ Now John also was baptizing at Aenon near Salim, because there was plenty of water, and people were coming and being baptized. ²⁴ (This was before John was put in prison.) ²⁵ An argument developed between some of John's disciples and a certain Jew over the matter of ceremonial washing. ²⁶ They came to John and said to him, "Rabbi, that man who was with you on the other side of the Jordan-the one you testified about-look, he is baptizing, and everyone is going to him."

²⁷ To this John replied, "A person can receive only what is given them from heaven. ²⁸ You yourselves can testify that I said, 'I am not the Messiah but am sent ahead of him.' ²⁹ The bride belongs to the bridegroom. The friend who attends the bridegroom waits and listens for him, and is full of joy when he hears the bridegroom's voice. That joy is mine, and it is now complete. ³⁰ He must become greater; I must become less."

READING

31

Much of your life you seek to build your own kingdom. You do work to make your name great and for you to be seen. When you seek to build a kingdom in your name you bring glory to yourself; this glory is built upon your performance and is temporal, it will not last. My kingdom is forever. My name is great and my glory eternal.

When you serve me and seek to bring glory to me, I increase and you decrease. This seems counter to everything you know. I know you are encouraged by the world that success is equal to a kingdom of fame.

Yet, when you bring me glory, you live in blessing and you share in an eternal inheritance that will always lead to joy.

And, it is my desire that you know joy. I am always leading you to life, the world will always lead you in the opposite direction. Choose to decrease, make me famous, and you will know the deepest joy you can imagine!

What do you hear?

LIVE

How will you respond?

A prompt for living

Boast and brag.

Today, be a storyteller who boasts in the Lord. Make a point to make Him famous in all of your conversation.

Make a point to share of His work in your life. Boast loudly and without shame.

LISTEN
John 3:31–34

³¹ The one who comes from above is above all; the one who is from the earth belongs to the earth, and speaks as one from the earth. The one who comes from heaven is above all. ³² He testifies to what he has seen and heard, but no one accepts his testimony. ³³ Whoever has accepted it has certified that God is truthful. ³⁴ For the one whom God has sent speaks the words of God, for God gives the Spirit without limit.

I speak to you with wisdom.

I speak to you with an eternal and purely good perspective.

I speak to you with grace.

I speak to you with truth.

I speak to you to reveal, not to hide.

I speak to you as your helper.

I speak to you as one who is for your good.

I speak to you for the good of all.

I speak to you words of love, grace, beauty, and human impossibility.

I speak to you often.

Often, you do not recognize my voice.

My voice makes little sense in the world, for the language of the world is in direct opposition to my words.

Listen to the words of life. Listen my child, hear me. I am always for you. I am always looking out for you. I will always care for you. Trust in this. Know this to be truth in the very depths of your heart and you will begin to recognize my voice.

Listen and obey.

When you do, when you choose to listen to words of life, you choose to walk with me and I promise you, I will always lead you to good.

Reading

32

What do you hear?

LIVE

How will you respond?

A prompt for living

Take a moment today to reflect on your life. Is there any place where you have been listening to the voice of the earth?

Ask God to show you what he has to say about the matter.

Respond to Holy Spirit's leading and do what he prompts.

LISTEN
John 3:35-36

³⁵ The Father loves the Son and has placed everything in his hands.
³⁶ Whoever believes in the Son has eternal life, but whoever rejects the Son will not see life, for God's wrath remains on them.

My son is salvation. In him you will find life and meaning and joy. I have placed everything in his hands.

I love you. I have given you the Son so that you will know life.

I have given you the Son so that you will have access to my kingdom.

I have given you the Son so that you will know to the fullest measure my goodness, truth, beauty, and grace.

I have given you the Son.

He is to be your very source of life.

Too often you look for life in other things. You desire the favorable opinion of others. You desire to be known, successful, and independent.

Your desire for intimacy often leads you to fill your life with idols: relationships, sex, and activities.

Your desires for safety and security sometimes take you to another set of idols: money, fences, rules, legalism, distrust, and weapons.

Your desires for success lead you to use people, lie, cheat, forget your family, push relationships aside, and large spheres of influence become your idol.

Every idol leads you away from life and towards death.

I am filled with anger for that which kills, steals, and destroys.

I sent my Son, to lead you towards life. Trust in Him. Follow Him. Believe in Him. And you . . . You will taste life and it will be deeply good.

What do you hear?

LIVE

How will you respond?

A prompt for living

What would it look like for you to be a conduit of God's life in one person?

Choose someone who is walking in a way contrary to the way of Jesus.

Do something for that person to encourage them, speak truth over them, or give to them. Pray that God will take your offering and expand its impact in that person's life for HIS kingdom good.

JOHN 4   (Readings 34–49)

READING

34

LISTEN
John 4:1-8

¹ Now Jesus learned that the Pharisees had heard that he was gaining and baptizing more disciples than John- ² although in fact it was not Jesus who baptized, but his disciples. ³ So he left Judea and went back once more to Galilee.

⁴ Now he had to go through Samaria. ⁵ So he came to a town in Samaria called Sychar, near the plot of ground Jacob had given to his son Joseph. ⁶ Jacob's well was there, and Jesus, tired as he was from the journey, sat down by the well. It was about noon.

⁷ When a Samaritan woman came to draw water, Jesus said to her, "Will you give me a drink?" ⁸ (His disciples had gone into the town to buy food.)

There is nothing accidental in your days.

Every moment of your day is filled with intention and possibility.

Each of your life's circumstances holds opportunity to serve, give, and breathe life into others. And, receive those things from me.

I care deeply about those I've lovingly created.

I care about your most basic needs and I will use every part of life, to bless you and to teach you.

Your choices matter. There are times where I lead you on journeys that make no sense to you. There are places I ask you to go that are outside of your comfort level. Step into these circumstances and trust my leading.

When you have need, bring it to me—even your most basic needs such as food and water. I desire to meet your need and use your need to lead you to be an encouragement to others.

Keep your eyes open, tell your story, speak to strangers, and look for evidence of me and my leading!

I will not waste any part of your life.

What do you hear?

LIVE

How will you respond?

A prompt for living

As you go about your everyday activities, look for ways to encourage, speak into, and give to others.

Do not plan an activity to do good, but look for opportunity as you are going and act upon the opportunity before you.

LISTEN
John 4:9

⁹ The Samaritan woman said to him, "You are a Jew and I am a Samaritan woman. How can you ask me for a drink?" (For Jews do not associate with Samaritans.)

I do not play favorites. My love is generous. I know that there are many who have been told that my love for them is contingent upon their birth, their behavior, or their belief. My love is not a respecter of persons.

My love is deep and it is generous.

I offer my love to every person, everywhere. But I do not force myself upon anyone. Generous love never forces itself on another. It simply loves and invites other to respond to that love.

Yes, my child, my love for you is rich. It stretches beyond the scope of your imagination. It reaches to the greatest heights and dwells in the lowest of valleys.

I invite you to my love.

I invite you to relationship with me.

I speak the first words and give my very presence as sign of my willingness to be where you are.

I sit with you. I walk with you. I offer myself to you, even when you feel unworthy.

Receive my gift today.

Receive my love.

And walk in it.

What do you hear?

LIVE

How will you respond?

A prompt for living

Imagine that you're hosting a party for every one of your friends. Who would you invite to the party?

Who would you not want at the party?

Make two lists.

Take the list of people you would not want at your party and choose one person from that list. Pray that God would increase your love for that person and do something this week to speak life over or serve them in some way.

LISTEN
John 4:10

[10] Jesus answered her, "If you knew the gift of God and who it is that asks you for a drink, you would have asked him and he would have given you living water."

I am the one who gives life. I am the one who fills you to the fullest measure. I am the one who replenishes your life source and fills your reservoir with reserves.

My life-giving flow is offered to you. Simply ask and I will cleanse you. I will renew you. I will wash over you. My living water is powerful.

My living water brings life to that which is seen and that which is unseen.

Your deepest sorrows. Your greatest pain. Your most shameful places and that which is hidden is met by me and I lovingly receive it all, washing over each part with grace,

love, beauty, and restoration. I promise, there will be no part of you left untouched by my life-giving truth and healing restoration.

I promise that your greatest sin is not too much for my living ways.

I promise that I will meet you and spill over you like a rushing river or bubbling brook, causing life to grow, where death once took hold.

Trust in me. Ask me for living water, and I will abundantly pour myself over you!

What do
you hear?

LIVE

How will you
respond?

A prompt
for living

Imagine Jesus is standing before you and he is asking you if you want living water.

Close your eyes and picture every sphere of your life. Imagine those places everyone sees and then move to that which only you know. Imagine your shame, hurt, anger, sadness, longings, and places that feel dead. Hold out your hands and ask for living water to flow over you.

Imagine what it feels like as Jesus pours this water and it hits what is cracked and dry. Imagine what it feels like as the water seeps in and replenishes that which is dead.

Imagine new life springing up in those places. What does it feel like? What does it look like?

Ask Jesus to bring life to that which is dead or hidden. Ask him to show you what it looks like to live out of his living water. And boldly choose life today.

LISTEN
John 4:11-14

11 "Sir," the woman said, "you have nothing to draw with and the well is deep. Where can you get this living water? 12 Are you greater than our father Jacob, who gave us the well and drank from it himself, as did also his sons and his livestock?"

13 Jesus answered, "Everyone who drinks this water will be thirsty again, 14 but whoever drinks the water I give them will never thirst. Indeed, the water I give them will become in them a spring of water welling up to eternal life."

I know that there are times where you doubt my care. I know that you come to me with concerns that are deep and troublesome. I know that you desire to live in light and life, yet at times it feels more like you live in darkness and death.

I give life. I give life that is full, abundant, and never ending. The life I offer you is complete. It enters into the very dark corners of your life and breathes over them. New life springs up from what was once dead and it refreshes that which once felt dry and barren.

My life is unfathomable. It comes in an instant and does not stop. My life is like a well that springs up to everlasting, ongoing, lavish, and outrageous life.

When you focus on the life I give, you walk in life, and it soothes and heals as you go.

Death is at your doorstep every day. Words that speak lies seeking to kill, steal, and destroy await you, but my life stands at the door to your heart and protects you from the darkness and the powers that are against you.

I long to give you life.

Receive my gift today.

And you shall live.

What do you hear?

LIVE

How will you respond?

A prompt for living

Do you know someone who is going through a difficult time?

Take a moment to pray that Jesus would show you words of life for him/her.

Write the person a card or stop by unannounced and communicate the words of life you were given for them.

Ask that Jesus would give you attentive ears to His life-giving words for others and speak them often and freely!

LISTEN
John 4:15

15 The woman said to him, "Sir, give me this water so that I won't get thirsty and have to keep coming here to draw water."

I do not give you life so that you can hide.

Yes, you have experienced much shame. You've kept secrets for years with fear of exposure. You hide in various activities: TV watching, game playing, working, serving, drinking, ministering, and exercise. You hide for fear that you would be too much or not enough for the world to handle or for me to love.

I know that you hide to self-preserve.

I know that there is shame and pain that keeps you from spending time with me and with others in true relationship.

This is why I invite you to life.

You do not believe that this offer is true. You question, "How can I get life when I've done or said or thought such things?"

You have not believed my offer to life is not attached to behavior.

I invite you to life not because of what you've done, but because I long to rescue you from the pain and isolation of hiding. My rescue is not conditional.

Yes, my dear one, I give you life. I am your rescue.

There is no need to hide. Simply receive and be amazed by the power of being seen.

Reading
38

What do you hear?

LIVE

How will you respond?

A prompt for living

Invite a person in your life to coffee or lunch who lives a way contrary to your belief / moral system.

Ask that God give you eyes to really see that person.

Through conversation, listen intently to their story, ask questions to understand, and invite that person to life in some way.

LISTEN
John 4:15-18

15 The woman said to him, "Sir, give me this water so that I won't get thirsty and have to keep coming here to draw water."
16 He told her, "Go, call your husband and come back."
17 "I have no husband," she replied. Jesus said to her, "You are right when you say you have no husband. 18 The fact is, you have had five husbands, and the man you now have is not your husband. What you have just said is quite true."

My ways are not your ways. My thoughts are not your thoughts.

There are times when you ask questions and it seems that my response to you is from left field, for you do not see how I see.

I know the depths of your circumstances and I call you out of every circumstance that is contrary to my best.

I speak to you the truth of your current situation.

I speak directly to your place of shame, but my words never add to your shame.

When I invite someone to repentance it is always, always, always in kindness. For it is kindness that leads to repentance.

You've come to believe that shame, accusation, and guilt are the expressions of my voice when I reveal what I see. This is a great lie of the enemy. It puts a wedge between us, and your belief that I speak to you in such a way, pushes you away from me and places you even deeper in the dark.

My voice of revelation, inviting to repentance will always be kind. My voice is like the warmth of the sun falling on you, revealing your shadow side.

I reveal the shadow with the warmth of light.

This light warms, heals, and restores as it reveals and it is good.

READING
39

What do
you hear?

LIVE

How will you
respond?

A prompt
for living

Ask Jesus to show you where you feel accused, shamed, or guilty.

Write out what comes to mind.

Tell the Lord that you've listened to and believed the voice of the enemy and ask that He'd show you His kindness.

Ask Jesus in what new way does He desire you to live.

Write what comes to mind. Respond with your life.

LISTEN
John 4:19-24

19 "Sir," the woman said, "I can see that you are a prophet. 20 Our ancestors worshiped on this mountain, but you Jews claim that the place where we must worship is in Jerusalem."

21 "Woman," Jesus replied, "believe me, a time is coming when you will worship the Father neither on this mountain nor in Jerusalem. 22 You Samaritans worship what you do not know; we worship what we do know, for salvation is from the Jews. 23 Yet a time is coming and has now come when the true worshipers will worship the Father in the Spirit and in truth, for they are the kind of worshipers the Father seeks. 24 God is spirit, and his worshipers must worship in the Spirit and in truth."

Your understanding of worship is limited by your traditions. You believe worship must look, sound, and feel a certain way. You subtly think that worship must take place in a certain setting. You have set ideas about how worship must be expressed for it to bless me. These ideas are often guided by your religious traditions, not a response to my way.

True worship takes place in the heart and is an act of the Spirit.

My beloved, this word is true. I do not long for songs in a particular key, played on a particular instrument. My beloved, I do not await hands raised and church pews full of attentive singers. Your songs and words and actions are meaningless if my Spirit is not in them.

I awaken you to truth, the truth of Me, and your response is your worship.

When you offer yourself, your whole self in response to my truth, it is your spirit worshipping.

Your life is the greatest gift of worship that you can give. It is costly. It is much more than a song. It is complete. It is beautiful; this spirit worship is beautiful to me. When your spirit receives mine and you live out of this truth it is the most fragrant aroma and offering you can lay before me.

Come, my child. Worship me, not with your words alone, but with your very life!

What do you hear?

LIVE

How will you respond?

A prompt for living

Invite a few friends over for dinner.

Create a discussion around the idea of worship.

(What is worship? Describe a worshipful experience. How is your life, your worship? What would it look like to live in such a way that increases your moment by moment worship?) Talk about these ideas and commit to putting some of them to practice over time.

LISTEN
John 4:25–26

25 The woman said, "I know that Messiah" (called Christ) "is coming. When he comes, he will explain everything to us."
26 Then Jesus declared, "I, the one speaking to you-I am he."

You often await a Savior. You have an idea of how he will look and you anticipate his coming. Fear grips you as you await his arrival. You grow impatient when you do not see the Savior of your circumstance or life situation in the form you believe saving should look.

You come to me and speak directly to me (your true salvation) about this coming salvation.

Though I am right before you, you cannot see.

Salvation has come to you.

Salvation is standing with you.

Salvation is ever before you.

Salvation is not something you anticipate, it is something you live in.

Salvation is found in me alone.

I find joy in revealing myself to you.

I delight in rescuing you from the enemy's voice.

I love to rescue you, my child.

When you look for salvation, look to me.

I am your salvation.

I have come.

READING
41

What do you hear?

LIVE

How will you respond?

A prompt for living

Visit a rescue mission and serve dinner or help in some way.

Ask Jesus to show you one person with whom you can connect through conversation. Ask if he/she would tell you their story and listen intently. As you listen, again, ask Jesus to show you where there is need for saving. Speak of the salvation of Jesus over that person. And share a time where you too have needed saving and how Jesus met you there.

LISTEN
John 4:27

27 Just then his disciples returned and were surprised to find him talking with a woman. But no one asked, "What do you want?" or "Why are you talking with her?"

You've heard it said that man looks at the outward appearance, but I look at the heart. This isn't just a nice sentiment; it is a deep truth. I see not your gender, race, fashion, ability, shape, or popularity. I look much past those things.

I see through you. I see your heart, your motivation, and your truest desires. These are the most intimate places within you.

When I see you, I see when you trust and you know peace. I see also when you fear and you are gripped by anxiety. I see your self-hatred which drives you to hide or judge and control others. I see also when your identity rests in me and you bring your whole self to others, inviting them to do the same.

I know you have been wounded by those who see only your shape, color, gender, and performance. I know that your heart aches for the approval of others. I know that you long to be truly seen and for your voice to be truly heard.

As I sit with you, I invite you to freedom from the opinion of others. I bring my whole self to you, and I ask you to do the same. When you find yourself in me, you will live out of a centered place, and your life will be an offering of worship to me. You will know, that I, the Creator of heaven and earth, hear and see you.

I love you.

READING

42

What do you hear?

LIVE

How will you respond?

A prompt for living

Host a dinner party.

Prepare a meal of your favorites. Choose things that allow the person/people you host to see you.

As the evening unfolds ask questions to get to know the inside of those who gather. Answer the questions truthfully yourself. Bring you and receive them!

LISTEN
John 4:28-30

28 Then, leaving her water jar, the woman went back to the town and said to the people, 29 "Come, see a man who told me everything I ever did. Could this be the Messiah?" 30 They came out of the town and made their way toward him.

Encounters with me are contagious.

When you experience the freedom of being truly seen and loved simultaneously, your life changes. The underlining belief that if someone were to find out the "truth," they would leave, no longer stands to reason. I have seen. I always see and I always love.

I see you, I know your whole story, I know your sin struggles and I see your deepest sorrows and I love you. Find your acceptance in me. I do not accept you because of what I see or don't see, no, I accept you because I created you.

Find joy in this acceptance.

As you do, you will not be able to keep silent. You will tell your story to any who will listen. You will run into the streets with pure joy. You will know freedom and that freedom will be contagious.

All will want to come to me to see if it is really true.

Can a person be fully seen and fully loved at the same time? The answer, when I am the one loving, is always a resounding YES!

Let this truth wash over you, and as you collide with this truth, take to the streets, and tell the world that you were truly seen and fully loved.

What do you hear?

LIVE

How will you respond?

A prompt for living

Choose one person with whom you've built a trusting relationship to share your story.

Share how God sees you and loves you. Do not be afraid or ashamed; simply share the story.

Ask God to make His name famous as you share and that He'd be contagious through your words!

LISTEN
John 4:31–34

31 Meanwhile his disciples urged him, "Rabbi, eat something."
32 But he said to them, "I have food to eat that you know nothing about."
33 Then his disciples said to each other, "Could someone have brought him food?"
34 "My food," said Jesus, "is to do the will of him who sent me and to finish his work.

Food is an everyday example of your frailty. You need food to survive. It is a fact. Without food, you would not live. In the same way water is a constant reminder of how you are dependent upon my creation to sustain life. Every time you eat and drink you are participating in the common activities of dependence.

Obedience is the food that gives life to your whole being. When you do my will, you sustain and even enhance life. As you listen to my voice, trust me and obey what I say.

Your obedience will bring about abundant life.

Without food and water you cannot sustain life, you grow weak, your body begins to break down and you soon will sit at death's doorstep. The same will happen when you are not obedient to my way and my will.

When you are disobedient, you grow tired, confused, anxious, and ultimately you grow frail. Death is ultimately the result of disobedience.

Because I am the creator of life, the source of life and the giver of life, I ALWAYS have life in mind as I speak with you. When I ask something of you, it is because I know where life is to be found and I invite you to join me.

Trust me in this, believe and receive the life that comes from obedience!

What do you hear?

LIVE

How will you respond?

A prompt for living

Bring a water bottle to work with you. Each time you take a drink, thank God for creating and sustaining your life.

Keep a crate of bottled water in your car and when you see a person who is asking for help, give them water and tell them, you pray that they'd encounter the Living water who desires to meet their every need.

LISTEN
John 4:35-38

³⁵ Don't you have a saying, 'It's still four months until harvest'? I tell you, open your eyes and look at the fields! They are ripe for harvest. ³⁶ Even now the one who reaps draws a wage and harvests a crop for eternal life, so that the sower and the reaper may be glad together. ³⁷ Thus the saying 'One sows and another reaps' is true. ³⁸ I sent you to reap what you have not worked for. Others have done the hard work, and you have reaped the benefits of their labor."

Partnership is a part of my kingdom that is deeply embedded and woven into its very fabric. I have created all of my children to participate in some way and each role is important.

At times you wonder why you've not done this or that. You've asked why you've not been the one to pray with others, speak to crowds, be the person others go to for comfort. You question whether or not your gift is enough.

I tell you the truth, the world is in need of your gift today. Your gift may be used to tell my story. Another's gift may be to see a person come to faith in me. Both gifts are needed and today is the day for you to walk in your unique make up and gifting.

Give of yourself to others for the benefit of my kingdom.

Give of yourself for my glory.

When you don't think your gift is enough or you covet the gifts of others, you are showing that you desire fame for yourself or you feel shame that you're not enough for me, both of these ideas do not hold truth and are not from me.

Use your gift today to speak, listen, sing, serve, give, love, touch, lead, restore, teach, comfort, protect, and invite. As you use the gifts I give you, you bring glory to me.

What do you hear?

LIVE

How will you respond?

A prompt for living

What special gift or talent do you posses?

Take a moment to think of one thing you know you do well or that which comes easily.

Have it? Now, think of a way you can use that gift to be an encouragement to others, then go and do it!

LISTEN
John 4:39-42

39 Many of the Samaritans from that town believed in him because of the woman's testimony, "He told me everything I ever did." 40 So when the Samaritans came to him, they urged him to stay with them, and he stayed two days. 41 And because of his words many more became believers.

42 They said to the woman, "We no longer believe just because of what you said; now we have heard for ourselves, and we know that this man really is the Savior of the world."

My child, I know you well. I see you in the morning and in the evening. I am with you throughout the day. My eyes are a witness to your life.

My love is as constant as my presence in your life.

I know when you fail, I love you.

I see when you respond to loneliness in ways that do not honor me, I love you.

I see when you lie to obtain approval, I love you.

I am a witness to your constant worry, I love you.

I am a witness to your scheming to get to the top, I love you.

I walk with you when you do not walk with me, I love you.

I walk with you when you trust yourself, over my truth, I love you.

I am intimately aware of your deepest pains and greatest joys. My love does not ebb and flow with your emotions and actions. My love is constant and my love invites you to live in truth and sight along with me.

When you believe that I see you as you are and love you, you know freedom because the truth always sets you free.

This freedom releases you from the captivity which holds you back and hides you. This freedom, my truth and love give, transforms you, and that transformation always invites others to me.

The truth sets you free, and it also bears witness of me to the world.

I long for every person everywhere to live in the truth and the reality of my love. Your transformed life will lead others to me.

READING
46

What do you hear?

LIVE

How will you respond?

A prompt for living

Think of a local spot (grocery store, coffee shop, street corner, diner . . . etc.) Who is the person who serves you most often in those places? Take time today to recognize him / her in some way. Write a card, bring a gift, or stop just to say thank you. Being seen is powerful. As you see others, you are inviting them into relationship and are also inviting them to see Jesus who is in you.

LISTEN
John 4:43-45

43 After the two days he left for Galilee. 44 (Now Jesus himself had pointed out that a prophet has no honor in his own country.) 45 When he arrived in Galilee, the Galileans welcomed him. They had seen all that he had done in Jerusalem at the Passover Festival, for they also had been there.

I watch as you are amazed by my marvelous works. You tell of my fame when I accomplish the miraculous in your life. You worship me when events unfold just as you asked. You worship me when your eyes see me at work and your life feels the effects of me working in it.

There are times though, when you do not feel me. Times when you wrestle with whether or not I am true or if I care. There are times when life simply goes by and you do not look for me.

It is my desire that you welcome me, whether you experience a miracle or whether you simply encounter my daily revelation through my creation. I never stop revealing myself. Every second of every day I am revealing myself. It is for you to experience!

You must not get so caught up in signs and wonders that you miss me. I desire for you to see me all over. To see me with your eyes and your heart. To experience me when you breathe and when you wake in the morning. Let the very small miracles of life point you to me. When the sun rises and the stars shine, think of me, that I am your light. When the trees bear fruit, remember that I created the fruit, and it was good.

Look for me today, every day. You will always find me.

What do you hear?

LIVE

How will you respond?

A prompt for living

Take five minutes today to reflect on the many ways God has revealed himself to you.

Make a list, draw a picture, or take a photo to capture that, which was revealed.

Now, make a point to share your list or part of it with someone in natural conversation. Simply bring it up, as if it were something you were thinking about today. Follow up by asking the person what the experience that is miraculous in their day.

LISTEN
John 4:46-50

⁴⁶ Once more he visited Cana in Galilee, where he had turned the water into wine. And there was a certain royal official whose son lay sick at Capernaum. ⁴⁷ When this man heard that Jesus had arrived in Galilee from Judea, he went to him and begged him to come and heal his son, who was close to death. ⁴⁸ "Unless you people see signs and wonders," Jesus told him, "you will never believe." ⁴⁹ The royal official said, "Sir, come down before my child dies." ⁵⁰ "Go," Jesus replied, "your son will live." The man took Jesus at his word and departed.

My dear one, my greatest desire is that you believe in me and my Son who I sent to you. I am life. I am salvation. I am healing. You need no sign or wonder to reveal to you, I am who I say I am. My invitation is that you believe and receive. Receive from me all that I give.

When you are burdened, believe that I hold the weight of your life.

When you are hopeless, believe that I am hope.

When you are alone, believe that I am with you.

When you are sick, believe that I am your healing.

I have given you life that is rich and full, a life that your earthly trials cannot take from you. Believe and receive. Have courage my dear one, in my very words, life itself is found.

READING
48

What do you hear?

LIVE

How will you respond?

A prompt for living

Where has the sting of death touched those around you? Take a moment to stop what you are doing and pray for life to come and fill the places touched by death. Write a text, card, or email, to encourage your friend with words of life.

LISTEN
John 4:51–54

51 While he was still on the way, his servants met him with the news that his boy was living. 52 When he inquired as to the time when his son got better, they said to him, "Yesterday, at one in the afternoon, the fever left him."

53 Then the father realized that this was the exact time at which Jesus had said to him, "Your son will live." So he and his whole household believed.

54 This was the second sign Jesus performed after coming from Judea to Galilee.

I am exact in my timing. I do everything with precise measure and attention. I am detailed in every sense of the word.

Pay close attention to the works of my hand.

Ask questions about time and place as these things truly matter in my kingdom.

There are no accidents in my kingdom. There are no happenstances.

Look for me and you will discover this to be true.

My child, there is no room for chance with me. Every person you meet, every financial provision, each burden placed on your heart or person suddenly coming to mind, those are all gifts from me and will lead to the encouragement of others and to the glory of my name. I love when your trust in me is deepened, therefore, I provide constant resources in your life to point you to me, my work, my timing, my answers, my provision, my way, and my constant knowledge of and presence in your life.

Trust me. Trust me with the impossible, the heavy, the confusion, the exciting, the deepest sadness. Trust me.

Trust me. I will be perfect in my response in every single way.

My love for you is greater than you can comprehend. My care for you is beyond understanding. I do hear you. I do see you. I am with you. Trust me and I will be seen in your life.

What do
you hear?

LIVE

How will you
respond?

A prompt
for living

Name one person you'd love to know Jesus. Write down their name, the date, the time, and their current circumstances. Start praying for this person to come to Jesus. Do not stop praying until you believe that God will answer this prayer. When you believe that he or she will come to Jesus, begin thanking God for their salvation.

Keep track of the details of this journey. Look for God's work in their life and write it down.

(This will take longer than a day, sometimes it takes years, but you can begin praying today. God will be detailed in this answer to prayer, you have to keep your eyes open to see!)

JOHN 5   (Readings 50–59)

LISTEN
John 5:1-7

¹ Some time later, Jesus went up to Jerusalem for one of the Jewish festivals. ² Now there is in Jerusalem near the Sheep Gate a pool, which in Aramaic is called Bethesda [a] and which is surrounded by five covered colonnades. ³ Here a great number of disabled people used to lie—the blind, the lame, the paralyzed. [4] [b] ⁵ One who was there had been an invalid for thirty-eight years. ⁶ When Jesus saw him lying there and learned that he had been in this condition for a long time, he asked him, "Do you want to get well? "Sir," the invalid replied, "I have no one to help me into the pool when the water is stirred. While I am trying to get in, someone else goes down ahead of me."

You are full of excuses. You say you believe and yet you give reasons to validate your non-belief. This is a difficult truth.

You want me to enter in to your life and your story and yet you push me away in the very same breath.

To take hold of me, my way, my truth, and my life, you must let go of yours. You must be willing to let go of your logic, reason, excuses, and behaviors that push me away.

Trust is the face of obedience.

When you trust that I am good, that I am faithful, your trust in me reveals itself as obedience. This is also true of your love for me. When you love me, you obey what I command.

Your obedience is the ultimate form of trust.

I do not long for your obedience because I'm power hungry. There is no need for me to hunger for power. No, I long for your obedience because I deeply love you. I created you and this earth and as the Creator I know what is good and right and perfect. Do trust me in this. I long for your obedience because I long for you to walk in freedom. I want you to let go of that to which you hold, to take hold of me, because I know you better than you know yourself.

Take hold of me and live out my way.

For I am good and right and perfect and desire all that is good and right and perfect for you my beloved.

What do you hear?

LIVE

How will you respond?

A prompt for living

What excuses do you make that keep you from obedience?

Ask God to show you what you need to let go of, to take hold of His way and life.

Write these things down.

Take a friend out for coffee and share your story and invite them to think of the same questions.

Discuss, pray, and encourage.

LISTEN
John 5:8-9

⁸ Then Jesus said to him, "Get up! Pick up your mat and walk." ⁹ At once the man was cured; he picked up his mat and walked.

When you experience my healing, it is yours to live. I have healed much of you. I've heard your prayers and have answered them. You often doubt my ability to heal, so instead of walking in freedom, you remain seated as though you are still awaiting my healing touch.

When I heal, I invite you to participate. I ask you to live into your healing. The evidence of healing is found in obedience.

Get up! Pick up the mat you've clung to, the home of pain and suffering on which you've lived and walk away. Leave this place and walk in freedom.

I do not heal so you can stay seated. I heal for your good and for the good of those around you. This means you must walk in your healing.

Trust is shown as you walk.

Today, trust me with your pain, anger, hurt, frustration, paralyzation, and weight—future and present. Trust me to heal you and pick up your mat and walk!

Reading
51

What do you hear?

LIVE

How will you respond?

A prompt for living

Write a letter to a friend you have been praying for and encourage them to believe and to walk.

LISTEN
John 5:8-13

8 Then Jesus said to him, "Get up! Pick up your mat and walk." 9 At once the man was cured; he picked up his mat and walked. The day on which this took place was a Sabbath, 10 and so the Jewish leaders said to the man who had been healed, "It is the Sabbath; the law forbids you to carry your mat."

11 But he replied, "The man who made me well said to me, 'Pick up your mat and walk.'"

12 So they asked him, "Who is this fellow who told you to pick it up and walk?"

13 The man who was healed had no idea who it was, for Jesus had slipped away into the crowd that was there.

I long for you to trust in all of my ways. I long for you to live in the miracle; to live in the freedom my love and grace and healing can bring. I long for you to celebrate the miracles I perform in others lives as well.

When one receives healing from past sin, do not wish for them to pay for it, celebrate with them.

When one finds freedom in me and expresses it in a way that clashes with human religious law and standard, do not judge them, rejoice that freedom has been found.

When one who was once bound by patterns of behavior is released from their grasp, do not envy my work in their life. No! Be glad and celebrate my perfect work

Rejoice when people find healing, restoration, grace, freedom, and life in me.

Rejoice! And again I say REJOICE!

Do not compare my work in your life with my work in the lives of others. For my grace is given individually and it looks differently for each of my children.

Therefore, rejoice and be glad whenever you see a transformed life. Praise me when others walk for the first time. Shout aloud that I am good and my work is perfect.

What do you hear?

LIVE

How will you respond?

A prompt for living

Think of a person who has recently experienced the grace of God in some way. Perhaps a huge answer to prayer. Maybe a miraculous life change.

Do something to celebrate this moment with him/her. Write a card, take a plate of cookies, make a phone call . . . do one thing to celebrate the work of God in his/her life.

14 Later Jesus found him at the temple and said to him, "See, you are well again. Stop sinning or something worse may happen to you." 15 The man went away and told the Jewish leaders that it was Jesus who had made him well. 16 So, because Jesus was doing these things on the Sabbath, the Jewish leaders began to persecute him. 17 In his defense Jesus said to them, "My Father is always at his work to this very day, and I too am working." 18 For this reason they tried all the more to kill him; not only was he breaking the Sabbath, but he was even calling God his own Father, making himself equal with God.

Let life be your way. My dear child, I will never force life upon you, I simply offer it to you out of my great love for you. Because I love you, I desire for you to taste and know that I am good, in all things, at all times. My goodness is also offered to you. You may choose to walk in it, take hold of it, and be guided by it. When my good, my love and life are your way, you too will know life. And this life, will be marked by my goodness and love.

My life and my good are continuing their work in the world and will not stop until the work is complete. There is nothing that can keep my work from finishing what it was set out to do. Trust in me, walk with me, and you will know life that is full of abundance. My dear child, choose life!

READING

53

**What do
you hear?**

LIVE

**How will
you respond?**

**A prompt
for living**

Access today's news by whatever means you can. As you read pray God's life and good over each situation. When one situation stands out to you more than another, take a moment and ask Jesus if there is an invitation for you in it? Make note of anything you hear or where you are prompted to pay extra attention. Pray over this place and these situations throughout your day.

LISTEN
John 5:19-20a

19 Jesus gave them this answer: "Very truly I tell you, the Son can do nothing by himself; he can do only what he sees his Father doing, because whatever the Father does the Son also does. 20 For the Father loves the Son and shows him all he does.

I have given you my whole self.
I have given you eyes with which you see,
ears with which you hear,
a heart with which you feel,
a mind with which you think and
a body with which you move.
I have given you myself and you have the honor of giving me to others with your life.
As you obediently follow me, you put my will and way into practice.

When you participate in my work, you share in the work of a grand kingdom.
It is my desire that you are intimately connected to me and keenly aware of my presence with you. As you are aware of my loving presence, I will make you aware of others.
I love you and those who surround you, therefore I will show you all I do and I will accomplish my will through you.
Listen. Believe. Receive. Follow.
I will show you a great way!

What do you hear?

LIVE

How will you respond?

A prompt for living

Go to a local gathering spot. (A local coffee shop, a strip mall, a pub or cafe . . .)

Sit in your car or as you walk to the location ask God to show you one need to which you can respond. Expect to see!

Pray that God will give you courage to speak and to act.

Take time to sit at your location interacting with others and look for God's spotlight, showing you a need to which you can respond. When a need is revealed to you, do something about it!

Tell someone of your experience and encourage them to go and do likewise.

LISTEN
John 5:20b-23

²⁰ Yes, and he will show him even greater works than these, so that you will be amazed. ²¹ For just as the Father raises the dead and gives them life, even so the Son gives life to whom he is pleased to give it. ²² Moreover, the Father judges no one, but has entrusted all judgment to the Son, ²³ that all may honor the Son just as they honor the Father. Whoever does not honor the Son does not honor the Father, who sent him.

It is not your responsibility to bring life to all things—that is the work of my Son who is in you. You belong to Him and he is at work in your life, bringing life to that which is around you. His Kingdom way is at work in you, and as you go through your day, you bring His life, goodness, truth, and beauty with you. This is not something that you put on as if a shirt in the morning, but it is something that you carry within you.

My beloved child, know that you are a conduit for my Son's life in the world. Receive his love, mercy, goodness, truth, and beauty, and then speak of it, share it, live out of it. Your life will bear the fruit, revealing your belief in Me and my Son . . . your life will bear the fruit of what you believe about yourself as a result.

Nestle into the love that I give you, let it surround you, and be the story your life speaks.

READING

55

What do you hear?

LIVE

How will you respond?

A prompt for living

Think of a place, a circumstance, or people in the world that need to experience goodness, truth, and beauty. Take some time to pray over what comes to mind, asking that God's kingdom come and his will be done in those places as it is in heaven. If there is a way to encourage or speak life into the circumstance, take time to do so today.

LISTEN
John 5:24-27

24 "Very truly I tell you, whoever hears my word and believes him who sent me has eternal life and will not be judged but has crossed over from death to life. 25 Very truly I tell you, a time is coming and has now come when the dead will hear the voice of the Son of God and those who hear will live. 26 For as the Father has life in himself, so he has granted the Son also to have life in himself. 27 And he has given him authority to judge because he is the Son of Man.

Listen closely.
I speak the very words of life.

Do you hear?

The very sound of my voice brings life.

When you walk through a day where your vision is blurred.

Listen closely.
When your dreams have been deterred.

Listen closely.
When your way does not make sense.

Listen closely.
When your circumstances overwhelm you.

Listen closely.
When your loved one is not well.

Listen closely.
When you're tired of waiting.

Listen closely.
When you've gone astray.

Listen closely.
When life seems upside and you cannot see my purpose or plan.

Listen closely.

It is true, when what is dead, broken, wounded, disheartened, frightened, alone, and aching, hears my voice, life springs up in the most surprising and unexpected ways.

I am standing with you in your circumstances. Take courage. For just as I've led you to where you are, I will lead you to what is next. Trust and listen.

What do you hear?

LIVE

How will you respond?

A prompt for living

Listen today to the words of those around you. When words of darkness, self doubt, self hatred, or gossip are spoken, make a point to pray and ask the Lord for words of life.

Speak those new words over the person or into the situation.

28 "Do not be amazed at this, for a time is coming when all who are in their graves will hear his voice 29 and come out—those who have done what is good will rise to live, and those who have done what is evil will rise to be condemned. 30 By myself I can do nothing; I judge only as I hear, and my judgment is just, for I seek not to please myself but him who sent me."

31 "If I testify about myself, my testimony is not true. 32 There is another who testifies in my favor, and I know that his testimony about me is true.

33 "You have sent to John and he has testified to the truth. 34 Not that I accept human testimony; but I mention it that you may be saved. 35 John was a lamp that burned and gave light, and you chose for a time to enjoy his light.

36 "I have testimony weightier than that of John. For the works that the Father has given me to finish-the very works that I am doing-testify that the Father has sent me.

As you go throughout life you look for many testimonies. You want others to confirm the work that I am about. You long to have human proof of my divine work.

When you see the sky. Worship me, the Creator.

When you experience healing. Worship me, the healer.

When you experience friendship. Worship me, the one who created relationship.

When you receive the needed resource. Worship me, the one who provides.

When you are lost. Worship me, the way.

When you see a shooting star. Worship me, the one who gives each star its home.

When you sit on the beach watching the waves crash. Worship me, the one who sustains the oceans.

When you listen to a masterful piece of music. Worship me, the one who created song.

Let all things point you to me.

You want to understand how all things came to be. You want to seek first the kingdom of man, so that you can have answers that fit into your understanding of how things are to be. Confess this attitude and worship me. I am the only word of proof you need.

What do you hear?

LIVE

How will you respond?

A prompt for living

Take a walk with a friend. Pray that God would give witness to himself as you walk. As you walk, point out the works of God. As you are going, be witness to the things of God.

LISTEN
John 5:27-40

37 And the Father who sent me has himself testified concerning me. You have never heard his voice nor seen his form, 38 nor does his word dwell in you, for you do not believe the one he sent. 39 You study the Scriptures diligently because you think that in them you have eternal life. These are the very Scriptures that testify about me, 40 yet you refuse to come to me to have life.

Wake Up! Do you not see that at times you worship the text of Scripture I've given you more than you worship me? The scriptures tell my story, they speak truth, and they are an important part of your life with me, but they are empty if you do not come to my Son for life. The scriptures themselves do not give life. No, it is only I who give life. I give life through my Son and he is the only way, truth, and life.

You listen to great teachers and you proclaim to follow their teaching. You attend churches and do not claim that the church is mine, but instead you claim the church by the person who speaks my words. You read books and get excited every time a new book comes out with an author of your liking.

Do you not see how ridiculous this all is? Without me, all of this is noise!

Wake Up! Do you not see that at times you do not hear my voice because you are not searching for me, but instead you are searching for what people have said concerning me? Come to my Son. His very name is salvation. He is life, for I have given him my life. Come to my Son to have life. Come to my Son to experience the life that I long to give you. Come to my Son.

**What do
you hear?**

LIVE

**How will
you respond?**

**A prompt
for living**

For one week, put away your Bible, don't listen to any sermons and don't read any books about God.

Ask God to reveal Himself to you through your everyday living—go to Him for life.

If a scripture comes to mind, visit it the following week—take walks—pray.

Use your senses and ask God, who is alive, to speak to you, and reveal Himself to you.

Share about this experience with someone in your life.

LISTEN
John 5:41–47

41 "I do not accept glory from human beings, 42 but I know you. I know that you do not have the love of God in your hearts. 43 I have come in my Father's name, and you do not accept me; but if someone else comes in his own name, you will accept him. 44 How can you believe since you accept glory from one another but do not seek the glory that comes from the only God?

45 "But do not think I will accuse you before the Father. Your accuser is Moses, on whom your hopes are set. 46 If you believed Moses, you would believe me, for he wrote about me. 47 But since you do not believe what he wrote, how are you going to believe what I say?"

You are quick to give glory to those on a big screen, those who can run fast, those who speak well, or have lots of money. You are quick to give glory to those who are published or discover cures for diseases. You are quick to give glory to those with extraordinary talent and those who can solve complicated problems.

You give glory to that which you see with your eyes and touch with your hands. You seek to align yourself with this glory and gain it for yourself.

Reading

59

In doing this you miss my glory though I need no screen, own all of the earth, created everything the earth holds, and am the solution to life's greatest problems. I created that which you discover, yet you seek the glory for yourself or give it to men and worship them.

I am by name glorious and it is my desire that you seek me. Align yourself with me and you will reveal my very glory through your life.

Quickly repent of your quest for human glory and your desire to align yourself with the famous of the earth. Turn then towards me, seek me. When you do so, you will find me, this is a promise.

What do you hear?

LIVE

How will you respond?

A prompt for living

When you find yourself envious of another's position, success, or popularity, immediately confess this and begin to pray for that individual. Pray that he/she would seek God's glory and that he would use you to be a part of revealing Himself to him/her.

JOHN 6   (Readings 60–78)

LISTEN
John 6:1-4

¹ Some time after this, Jesus crossed to the far shore of the Sea of Galilee (that is, the Sea of Tiberias), ² and a great crowd of people followed him because they saw the signs he had performed by healing the sick. ³ Then Jesus went up on a mountainside and sat down with his disciples. 4 The Jewish Passover Festival was near.

You see me do miraculous things. You know I am capable of healing the sick, providing at the perfect time, giving words for the broken, and leading you to the exact spot where you'll thrive. You know that I am good and that I look out for you and am with you. You believe with all of your heart and mind that I am God.

I watch as you desire for others to know this truth as well. I see you want to convince others. I hear your prayers on behalf of the hurting. I know your deep trust. Your faith does not fall on blind eyes or deaf ears.

I know you love me. And, my dear one, at times you bear a weight that is not yours to bear. You carry the weight of prayers. You bear the burden of the broken, the sick, the outcast. You grieve for the lost. You cry out for the hurting.

And, you can get so busy doing work, carrying burdens and crying out, that you forget to come to me. You work for me rather than believe in me. It is not your work that I want, it is your heart and your belief in me. I want time with you because I want to be with you. I love when you go to the mountainside to be alone with me. I love when you give up your working for a time to deepen your relationship with me, the one who actually causes your work to have impact.

Come to me with that with which you carry and trust that I will carry it well. Come to me with your heart and I will breathe life into it. Come to me with your belief and I will increase it.

I love you my dear child. Trust this and come away with me for no other reason, but to be with the one you love.

**What do
you hear?**

LIVE

**How will
you respond?**

**A prompt
for living**

Go away to a secret place to be with Jesus.

⁵ When Jesus looked up and saw a great crowd coming toward him, he said to Philip, "Where shall we buy bread for these people to eat?" ⁶ He asked this only to test him, for he already had in mind what he was going to do.

My beloved, there are times when trials and impossibilities confront you and you wonder what you are to do. Human trails are not impossible for me, nor are they inconvenient, nor are they trials at all. Human trials are always an invitation to trust.

When impossibility confronts you, I place a question on your mind, "What am I to do?"

I know the answer.

But I pose the question as an opportunity to trust.

When you face impossibility, what are you to do?

May your response always be, "Lord, I believe you are good. I desire to follow your way. I believe you are sovereign. I believe this is an opportunity to trust. Therefore, I choose to trust you. You will make a way for me."

I will make a way for you.

You are my beloved and I will never leave you hanging or place you in the midst of trails that I cannot overcome.

Every trial, every situation of impossibility, every moment of uncertainty is an invitation to trust.

My beloved, respond to the invitation and trust me today.

**What do
you hear?**

LIVE

**How will
you respond?**

**A prompt
for living**

Do you have a friend going through a difficult time? Facing a trial? Confronted with impossibility?

Write them a card today to remind them that God is the God of impossibilities and that He will do what is good for them.

LISTEN
John 6:7-11

⁷ Philip answered him, "It would take more than half a year's wages to buy enough bread for each one to have a bite!" ⁸ Another of his disciples, Andrew, Simon Peter's brother, spoke up, ⁹ "Here is a boy with five small barley loaves and two small fish, but how far will they go among so many?"¹⁰ Jesus said, "Have the people sit down." There was plenty of grass in that place, and they sat down (about five thousand men were there). ¹¹ Jesus then took the loaves, gave thanks, and distributed to those who were seated as much as they wanted. He did the same with the fish.

Yes, I am the God of impossibilities.

There is nothing out of my capable hands.

When faced with an impossible challenge you have a choice to either become paralyzed by the scale of the situation and your own lack of ability to meet the need. Or, you can bring to me what you have and trust that I can make something great of it.

I have given you everything you need. I've given you resources that you know nothing of. I have given you provision beyond your wildest imagination.

It is my desire that you trust me with impossibilities. Trust that although the situation is impossible to you, it is possible with me. When you face impossibility, respond with thanksgiving. Thank me for what I am about to do. Thank me for an opportunity to see me work. Thank me for my provision. Thank me for my all powerful nature. Thank me for my faithfulness in your past. Thank me for my current provisions and my future care.

Thank me and watch. Watch me meet your need.

Watch me answer your prayers. Watch me take what you have and multiply it to abundantly care. I will hear your prayer. I will meet your need.

Thank me and watch.

What do you hear?

LIVE

How will you respond?

A prompt for living

Is there a situation in your city, neighborhood, family, or community that weighs heavily on your heart? Does it seem impossible to see God's provision in it?

Thank God for who He has been and who He is.

Pray for this situation every day. Pray until you believe that God will meet the need and care for this situation. Ask him to give you eyes to see what you have to offer and then offer what you have. Watch!

Thank God for meeting this need and keep track of how he does so.

When the situation is healed or the need met, write a letter to those affected and tell them how you prayed and what you saw God do.

LISTEN
John 6:12-13

¹² When they had all had enough to eat, he said to his disciples, "Gather the pieces that are left over. Let nothing be wasted." ¹³ So they gathered them and filled twelve baskets with the pieces of the five barley loaves left over by those who had eaten.

I am an extravagant God.

There are times when I answer your prayers with such abundance that it is laughable and increases your faith. These times also are a part of declaring my name throughout all creation.

There are times when my extravagance is found in that which is hidden. I've allowed my people to come to a place of desperation before I met them with abundant resources. I've allowed my people to hit a wall that was impossible to overcome before I tore it down. I've allowed my people to be stopped in their tracks by a rushing river or vast sea before I parted the waters and kept them from flowing.

Over and over I brought my people to a place of great dependence.

And over and over I met them there and rescued them with such extravagance that there was no question who was the Savior.

I bring you, at times, to a place of desperation. I bring you to a place where you have no way out. I bring you to a place where you must depend on me.

At that time, I will come with such abundance that you can do nothing but look up to the heavens and laugh out loud.

My child I want to give you more than you can ask or imagine. Trust this as you step into the desperate times. Trust that my extravagance will meet you and be your rescue. There is no need to fear.

What do you hear?

LIVE

How will you respond?

A prompt for living

Listen. Take time to listen your friends and those around you. Listen to their stories and search out hints of desperation.

When you discover desperate hearts, pray for God's miraculous intervention and do whatever you can to encourage in the waiting. Be a conduit for God's encouraging presence as you wait alongside of another for God's abundant provision.

LISTEN
John 6:14-15

[14] After the people saw the sign Jesus performed, they began to say, "Surely this is the Prophet who is to come into the world." [15] Jesus, knowing that they intended to come and make him king by force, withdrew again to a mountain by himself.

You seek human approval and credit. You seek power and control. You want the final say and authority that man gives.

When this desire comes over you flee to the mountain.

When you desire to be seen and heard. Flee to the mountain.

When you think you're way is always best. Flee to the mountain.

When you struggle to submit. Flee to the mountain.

When you judge another's way because it's different than yours. Flee to the mountain.

When others put you in a place of ultimate authority. Flee to the mountain.

When others begin to follow you as their perfect example. Flee to the mountain.

Come to the mountain and be reminded that it is only I who is good and right and perfect.

Come to the mountain and submit to my loving care.

Submit to my power.

Submit to my authority.

Submit to my way.

Come to the mountain to receive all that I have to give. For I am good and right and perfect, my way is always wise, and my power is never lacking.

* Come to the mountain and be with me.

What do you hear?

LIVE

How will you respond?

A prompt for living

Who follows you?

Is it a friend, a member of your team, a student in your youth group, a mentee, a member of your church, a sibling, or a young person who looks up to you?

Take the opportunity to pray for this person. Pray that God would be the ultimate authority in their life.

Pray that you would handle your position in their life wisely.

Next time you are in conversation with them, encourage them to seek Jesus and his way. Make a point to let this person know that you submit to the way of Jesus because only he is good and right and perfect.

READING

64

LISTEN
John 6:16-21

16 When evening came, his disciples went down to the lake, 17 where they got into a boat and set off across the lake for Capernaum. By now it was dark, and Jesus had not yet joined them. 18 A strong wind was blowing and the waters grew rough. 19 When they had rowed about three or four miles, they saw Jesus approaching the boat, walking on the water; and they were frightened. 20 But he said to them, "It is I; don't be afraid." 21 Then they were willing to take him into the boat, and immediately the boat reached the shore where they were heading.

Do not be afraid.

I know that life is full of overwhelming situations.

I know that at times the lies of the enemy are so loud that it feels as though he will take you over.

What do you hear?

I know troubles come like the wind and rain creating rough waters that consume you.

I know that there are times when you feel I've forgotten you. Do not believe this to be true.

LIVE

Do not be afraid.

I accompany you. I am your constant companion. Though, at times you do not recognize me. And, at times you can be fearful, not realizing it is I.

How will you respond?

Take the bold step and invite me into your troubled places.

Invite me to join you on the rough waters.

Invite me to be the voice that overpowers the voice of the enemy.

Invite me in.

I promise that when you invite me into your situation, I will bring calm. I will lead you to your destination. I will be your ever-present help in times of trouble.

A prompt for living

Go to a place in your community where great needs abound. (There are many from which to choose)

Take a prayer walk around the neighborhood, building, or residence.

Pray blessing over the place. Pray that God will bless all comings and goings. Pray that God blesses the work of people's hands. Pray that God will bless all who live and work within these quarters. Whatever pops into your mind to pray blessing over, do it!

Do not be afraid. Invite me in.

I will be your calm.

As you pray blessing, ask God how you might be a blessing today. Whatever comes to mind at that moment, do it! Bring peace.

LISTEN
John 6:22-24

22 The next day the crowd that had stayed on the opposite shore of the lake realized that only one boat had been there, and that Jesus had not entered it with his disciples, but that they had gone away alone. 23 Then some boats from Tiberias landed near the place where the people had eaten the bread after the Lord had given thanks. 24 Once the crowd realized that neither Jesus nor his disciples were there, they got into the boats and went to Capernaum in search of Jesus.

People love a good story. People love to be amazed. People love sensationalized situations. You are drawn to such things without your knowledge.

The crowds were amazed by the works of my Son and chased after him. They wanted to see more. They wanted free food. They wanted to find him, not for who he was, but for what he could do for them.

There are times in your relationship with me where you desire what I can do for you more than you desire me. You grow envious of those who encounter me in miraculous ways. You desire to share in my grander and the marvelous works of my hands, often more than you desire me.

I do love to give good gifts to my children.

I love to abundantly give to you.

I give for your good and out of my love for you.

Be careful to not love the things I do for you more than me. When your worship turns from me to that which I can give or do, you have lost sight of me and serve an idol of miracles and wonders.

Be aware of your propensity to act in this way and keep your eyes steady on me. I am the author of your faith, and I am the one true God who is worthy of all honor and praise.

What do you hear?

LIVE

How will you respond?

A prompt for living

Make a list of that which the Lord has done for you. Once you've completed your list take time to reflect on how each answer to prayer or miracle point to the character of God. Write the coinciding character quality next to each answer or miracle.

Choose one that is most meaningful and share it with someone.

Celebrate God together!

25 When they found him on the other side of the lake, they asked him, "Rabbi, when did you get here?"

26 Jesus answered, "Very truly I tell you, you are looking for me, not because you saw the signs I performed but because you ate the loaves and had your fill. 27 Do not work for food that spoils, but for food that endures to eternal life, which the Son of Man will give you. For on him God the Father has placed his seal of approval."

I have watched you work, labor, and painstakingly seek to accomplish many tasks. You've strained yourself trying to figure the exact work to which you should give your life. I have heard your cries and seen your tears.

They do not miss my divine presence.

Today I ask you a new question.

Why is it that you work? To what end?

The answer to this question is crucial.

You either toil for that which perishes or for eternal things; things that ultimately give me glory and you life.

Often your labor is for comfort, prestige, or felt security.

Other times your labor is for provision, safety, or happiness.

Labor to these ends will never satisfy.

You'll arrive at your chosen destination only to realize that you feel as empty as you did prior to your labor.

Your work is important.

Your work is crucial.

It is necessary.

Yet, the end to which you arrive is the most important thing.

Make me your end game. Make me the object of your affection. Do not labor in vain for one more minute!

What do you hear?

LIVE

How will you respond?

READING
67

A prompt for living

Instead of working to please your boss, wife, husband, self, family etc. today, take a moment to visualize Jesus being the end game for your day.

Pray that God would increase your belief and trust in him and serve to honor the Lord throughout your day instead of serving any other thing.

Pay attention to how you feel, what you think, what prompts to action you experience.

Choose to act in response to these things.

LISTEN
John 6:28-29

28 Then they asked him, "What must we do to do the works God requires?"
29 Jesus answered, "The work of God is this: to believe in the one he has sent."

The work that man requires seeks to accomplish tasks for self advancement, care for needs, and to earn standing.

I do not work in the same way.

The work man requires places man as the ultimate provider.

The work I require places me as the ultimate provider.

Therefore, The work I seek from you is the hard work of belief.

Your work is simply to believe in the one I sent.

That is it—Believe.

Your work is not to advance my kingdom, no, it's to believe I'm capable of advancing my own kingdom through my Son.

Your work is not to bring people to salvation, no, it's to believe that my Son is salvation and believe that he will save your loved ones.

Your work is not to care for the hearts of people, no, it's to believe in the one who came out of great love for you and to believe that he will care for people.

Your work is not to serve, no, it's to believe in the one who came to seek and serve and to believe that he will serve others.

Your work is not found in your actions.

Your actions are a response to the hard work of belief.

Belief matters. It is your most sacred task.

You must believe that I sent my Son for you.

You must believe that I am the ultimate provider.

You must Believe, for it is the only work I require.

READING

68

What do you hear?

LIVE

How will you respond?

A prompt for living

Think of an impossible situation in a friend's life. In your life?

Pray for God to intervene.
Pray until you believe He will.

When you believe God will intervene, thank him in advance for His good work.

Do this in secret and watch your attitude change and your belief increase.

LISTEN
John 6:30-33

READING

69

³⁰ So they asked him, "What sign then will you give that we may see it and believe you? What will you do? ³¹ Our ancestors ate the manna in the wilderness; as it is written: 'He gave them bread from heaven to eat.' "

³² Jesus said to them, "Very truly I tell you, it is not Moses who has given you the bread from heaven, but it is my Father who gives you the true bread from heaven. ³³ For the bread of God is the bread that comes down from heaven and gives life to the world."

What do you hear?

Life and substance and provision are mine to give. I care for the earth and all its inhabitants. At times I accomplish my work through people, like you. Other times I accomplish this work without your participation.

I am the only one who gives life to the world.

I am the source of all miracles and provisions.

I am your source.

There are times when you confuse me with your work, those who serve you, and those who do my work around the world.

Do not be mistaken, I am the source of your provision.

Come to me when you need help.

Come to me when you don't have what it takes.

Come to me when you are up against a wall.

Come to me when you feel desperate.

Come to me and I will give you life.

I will be your source.

I will be your ever-present help in times of trouble.

For, I am, is my name, and I am with you.
I am for you.
I am your provision, help, miracle, and nourishment.

This is a truth you can count on.

LIVE

How will you respond?

A prompt for living

Throw a dinner party for some friends.

Before anyone arrives, think of a time when you experienced the miraculous provision of Jesus.

As you sit down to eat, thank the Lord for being your provision.

Then take time to share your story of a time when Jesus provided for you, miraculously.

Invite people to share experiences when they too had a need that was miraculously met.

LISTEN
John 6:34-35

34 "Sir," they said, "always give us this bread." 35 Then Jesus declared, "I am the bread of life. Whoever comes to me will never go hungry, and whoever believes in me will never be thirsty.

Your most basic provisions are met in me, I am their source. I am that which sustains you.

I am that which gives you life.

I am.

Because I am, there is no reason for you to hunger or thirst. These most basic needs are met in me.

I desire for you to live with this understanding.

It really does change the way you live.

It will change the way you interact with the world and your stress level.

You become worried about many things. Come to me with your worry and confess it.

Do not worry about anything, what you should eat or what you should drink. Do not exhaust yourself with anxiety.

Confess this to me and believe that I am the sustainer of your life.

Your belief in me will result in a life that is filled with peace, even in the midst of strenuous circumstances.

I am the bread of life, whoever comes to me will never go hungry, whoever believes in me will never be thirsty.

Let this truth be your constant encouragement and hope.

What do you hear?

LIVE

How will you respond?

A prompt for living

Create a practice; before you eat, take time to recognize God is the source of all life. Thank Him for giving you life and for one way you experienced life in your day. Invite those at your table to do the same.

36 But as I told you, you have seen me and still you do not believe. 37 All those the Father gives me will come to me, and whoever comes to me I will never drive away. 38 For I have come down from heaven not to do my will but to do the will of him who sent me. 39 And this is the will of him who sent me, that I shall lose none of all those he has given me, but raise them up at the last day. 40 For my Father's will is that everyone who looks to the Son and believes in him shall have eternal life, and I will raise them up at the last day."

My beloved, you are under my watchful care. My son has come, out of love, to be your rescue. It is my will that he never lose sight of you. You are a part of a great family and a rich inheritance.

When you believe in my Son, you experience life eternal. This life cannot be taken from you by any source, not even the grave.

Do not be discouraged.

Do not be afraid.

Do not fear abandonment.

You will never be taken from my care.

Let your hope rest in my Son, who will do what he says he will do.

You will never be abandoned.

You will not be forgotten.

I do not over promise and under deliver.

I am always true to my word.

Therefore, let your hope be secure. Let your spirit be at peace and may your heart be overwhelmed by my great love for you.

**What do
you hear?**

LIVE

**How will
you respond?**

**A prompt
for living**

Pray that God would remind you of a person in your life who needs to be reminded that they are cared for and loved by God. (Don't over think it, take the first name that came to mind.)

Write this person a letter describing God's great love and care for them. Mail it!

Pray that God will speak through your letter to encourage, strengthen faith, and deepen understanding.

LISTEN
John 6:41-43

⁴¹ At this the Jews there began to grumble about him because he said, "I am the bread that came down from heaven." ⁴² They said, "Is this not Jesus, the son of Joseph, whose father and mother we know? How can he now say, 'I came down from heaven'?" ⁴³ "Stop grumbling among yourselves,"

There are those who miss me because they seek me with human understanding.

Human understanding is limited to human experience.

I am beyond human logic.

I am outside of human experience.

When you grapple with things of my kingdom, with your mind, at times you will not understand.

Miracles are not meant to be understood, they are meant to be experienced.

You have the propensity to worship your mind. If you cannot understand something with human logic, then often it ceases to be true for you. This gets in the way of relationship with me, for I work outside of human logic and experience.

When things are outside of your logic and your understanding, worship me. Turn to me and express your lack of understanding and then choose to trust in me and step with obedience.

I will always work for your good.

Trust this as I invite you to live, at times, outside of human logic and responsibility.

Reading

72

What do you hear?

LIVE

How will you respond?

A prompt for living

Be a miracle for someone.

Pray that God will put an issue, person, or circumstance on your heart. Pay close attention as you go throughout your day. Does that issue come up in conversation? Does the person you're praying for call or do you bump into them. Listen with every one of your senses. Then act. Does something come to mind as a way to serve or give? Put it into practice!

LISTEN
John 6:44-46

[44] "No one can come to me unless the Father who sent me draws them, and I will raise them up at the last day. [45] It is written in the Prophets: 'They will all be taught by God.' Everyone who has heard the Father and learned from him comes to me. [46] No one has seen the Father except the one who is from God; only he has seen the Father.

I am constantly teaching you.

I am teaching those you love as well. You expect that I teach people through a particular church or organization, but I am not bound by human structures.

I teach people about me through nature.

I teach principles of restoration through rehab programs.

I teach people aspects of my character through many religions.

I have been known to use unnamed god's to prepare the way for someone to meet Jesus.

I prepare the way.

I lead people to my Son.

I am not afraid to use the things of man to ready someone's heart to receive my Son.

Do not be surprised if people find my Son through unlikely circumstances.

When this happens, praise me!

This is evidence that I have been teaching and leading.

I am willing to use whatever it takes to prepare a heart to receive my Son.

Look for me when others speak of beliefs, ideas, gods, and practices. Use these concepts to introduce my Son, pray that I will give them eyes to see and a heart to receive him.

It is not yours to convince. It is yours to declare.

I am constantly teaching, so trust that I will lead one to my Son and then look for ways to be a part of the introduction.

What do you hear?

LIVE

How will you respond?

A prompt for living

Listen carefully in conversation with friends who do not follow Jesus.

When you hear any hint of truth in an idea or belief that could be an avenue to speak of Jesus, bravely speak of Jesus, making an introduction.

(Become a person who is a scout for truth in other's stories. God uses many things to teach people about Himself, preparing the way for one to meet Jesus. You must listen for truth, this is a crucial part of your witness.)

READING
73

LISTEN
John 6:47–51

47 Very truly I tell you, the one who believes has eternal life. 48 I am the bread of life. 49 Your ancestors ate the manna in the wilderness, yet they died. 50 But here is the bread that comes down from heaven, which anyone may eat and not die. 51 I am the living bread that came down from heaven. Whoever eats this bread will live forever. This bread is my flesh, which I will give for the life of the world."

I am the source of life. Life is my name.

I give life to you through my Son.

It is my desire that all may live, not simply for today alone, but for eternity.

I am your daily sustainer and provider. I care deeply for your life to be whole and full and good. These things are true, but my truest desire is that you would know life beyond your earthly days.

READING

74

Come to my Son.

Receive him. Just as the Israelites received manna from heaven that gave life while they were in the desert, I have given you my Son, who came down from heaven so that you might have life, eternal life.

His very body is the source of your eternal provision.

You fear death. You spend money and time protecting yourself from death's grasp. You entrust your life to the things of men to keep from death's door, yet you ignore my Son.

Run from this. Turn from your worship of earthly life and invest yourself in the reality of my kingdom found in my Son. Oh my child, please come. Come to my Son. Run to him. Run to life. Run to good. Run, don't turn back. Don't look away. Run . . . as fast as you can, run to Jesus, my Son. And you will from that moment on, know eternal life.

What do you hear?

LIVE

How will you respond?

A prompt for living

Grab a few friends and visit a local hospital or elderly care facility. Bring with you a card and some flowers. Write a message of true life in the card.

Ask the staff which of the patients or residents has not had a visitor in the past week.

Go to that room and introduce yourself and ask if it'd be okay if you'd sit with them for a bit.

(Of course be very sensitive to the person's condition)

Give the card and flowers and explain that you came to remind them that they are not alone and that they have not been forgotten.

If you feel prompted to do so, ask if you can come back again to visit.

Pray that God uses your obedience to be a blessing and to point one toward real life.

LISTEN
John 6:52-59

52 Then the Jews began to argue sharply among themselves, "How can this man give us his flesh to eat?" 53 Jesus said to them, "Very truly I tell you, unless you eat the flesh of the Son of Man and drink his blood, you have no life in you. 54 Whoever eats my flesh and drinks my blood has eternal life, and I will raise them up at the last day. 55 For my flesh is real food and my blood is real drink. 56 Whoever eats my flesh and drinks my blood remains in me, and I in them. 57 Just as the living Father sent me and I live because of the Father, so the one who feeds on me will live because of me. 58 This is the bread that came down from heaven. Your ancestors ate manna and died, but whoever feeds on this bread will live forever." 59 He said this while teaching in the synagogue in Capernaum.

You worry about what you should eat. You spend a lot of time thinking about how your food will affect your body.

You've heard it said "you are what you eat." This is not only true with your physical body. This is also true with your spiritual body.

Therefore, feed your body, mind, heart, and spirit with things of me. Feed upon my Son. Allow him to be your daily nurturance. Find your sustenance in him.

Draw from the energy he provides.

The products of feeding on him are love, joy, peace, patience, kindness, goodness, gentleness, and self-control. These are the fruit of a life that feeds upon my Son.

Rid yourself of the junk food on which you've fed yourself for years and bite into the daily bread sent from heaven.

What do you hear?

LIVE

How will you respond?

A prompt for living

Choose life intentionally for one week. Choose life in what you eat, how you spend your time and how you speak. Pray that God will give you belief that Jesus is life and in him you find the ability to choose Jesus and life over things that temporarily feel good.

For one week fast from junk food. Replace the junk food with good, natural, organic food. As people notice your new eating habits and ask about it, tell them that you are want to feed your body life in all ways. Include in the conversation how you find life in Jesus for your whole well-being.

LISTEN
John 6:60-65

60 On hearing it, many of his disciples said, "This is a hard teaching. Who can accept it?" 61 Aware that his disciples were grumbling about this, Jesus said to them, "Does this offend you? 62 Then what if you see the Son of Man ascend to where he was before! 63 The Spirit gives life; the flesh counts for nothing. The words I have spoken to you-they are full of the Spirit and life. 64 Yet there are some of you who do not believe." For Jesus had known from the beginning which of them did not believe and who would betray him. 65 He went on to say, "This is why I told you that no one can come to me unless the Father has enabled them."

I am aware of you at all times.

I am aware of your comings and goings.

I am aware of your struggles with sin and addiction.

I am aware of your secret sorrows.

I am aware of your thoughts and unspoken words.

I am aware of your attitudes and every action.

I am deeply aware of your shame.

I am aware of your longings for freedom.

I am aware of your lack of belief.

I am aware of your faith.

I am aware of where you place your identity.

I am aware of when you depend on me and when you depend on self.

I am very aware. All of the time.

This awareness is not that of a policing father seeking to collect information to shame his children into submission or morality.

No, that is not a part of me. My awareness is that of a father who loves his children so deeply that he watches over them and constantly invites them to life.

There are times when you choose life and there are times when you choose to betray the way of life, the way of my Son.

Oh, my beloved child, know that I am aware and know that each prompting and invitation to life you encounter is for your good and will always result in life.

READING
76

What do you hear?

LIVE

How will you respond?

A prompt for living

Ask God to give you eyes with which you can see others. Ask that He would make you aware of one person. Throughout the day, when you notice this person be kind, encourage them. If you notice tension, pray for them. If you notice tears, go to them and let them know they are not alone. Make them aware that you notice them.

If they ask how you noticed or why you care, speak to God's loving awareness in your own life.

LISTEN
John 6:66

66 From this time many of his disciples turned back and no longer followed him.

I experience grief when you decide to turn from me.

My way is simple for those who trust me and believe that I am good.

My way seems impossible, even foolish to those who do not believe that I am good.

My child, you go back and forth with your faithfulness to me. There are times when you trust and your faith grows. There are times when life throws you a curve ball and you are stretched in faith and you choose worry and work as your companions, thus turning from me.

This grieves me, for I know what life is like without me and I feel the loss of your close relationship with me.

When you experience difficulty, cling to me, do not run! Cling.

Press into me, ask me questions, be honest with your disappointment, shame, worry, and cares.

Tell me that the teaching is hard.

Fill me in on your heart ache.

Tell me about the loss you experience, yell, scream, and cry out!

As you do so, your faith will increase, your life will know freedom and you will eventually become aware of my presence.

What do you hear?

LIVE

How will you respond?

A prompt for living

Be an extension of God's love to a friend who seemingly severed relationship with God when life became very difficult for them.

Ask God to give you one practical way to bless this friend today and then do it!

67 "You do not want to leave too, do you?" Jesus asked the Twelve.

68 Simon Peter answered him, "Lord, to whom shall we go? You have the words of eternal life. 69 We have come to believe and to know that you are the Holy One of God."

70 Then Jesus replied, "Have I not chosen you, the Twelve? Yet one of you is a devil!" 71 (He meant Judas, the son of Simon Iscariot, who, though one of the Twelve, was later to betray him.)

READING

78

I continually give invitations to trust.

In the garden I placed a tree, having given the instructions not to eat of its fruit. The tree was an invitation to trust.

I gave Abraham a vision and invited him to participate in it. The vision was an invitation to trust.

I brought my people to the edge of the Sea with the enemy pressing in. Their impossible situation was an invitation to trust.

I commanded my people to gather enough food to eat for a day's provision, when manna and quail were given in the wandering years. Each time they gathered, they were invited to trust.

I brought my people across the river and to a great city. I gave them victory over the city. Both the river and the city were invitations to trust.

David was the smallest of his family, yet he decided to fight the great giant. The giant was an invitation to trust.

Esther was placed in a palace and was given to a king as his bride. She was to prompted to risk her life to speak up for my people. Esther's prompting was an invitation to trust.

Jeremiah was given words from me to speak. The people did not like his words. My words to Jeremiah were an invitation to trust.

Daniel was told not to pray or he'd end up in a den of lions. The threat was an invitation to trust.

Shadrach, Meshach, and Abednego were commanded to worship an idol or they'd be thrown into a fiery furnace. The command was an invitation to trust.

Nehemiah was given the vision to rebuild the walls of Israel's home while he was in captivity. The vision and ask to rebuild were both invitations to trust.

From the beginning of time I have invited my people to trust in my character and respond with their lives.

I gave my Son as an invitation to trust.

Trust Him. Follow Him. For I am a Holy Good God, whose invitation to trust is always motivated by love.

What do
you hear?

LIVE

How will
you respond?

A prompt
for living

Write down the invitations to trust you've experienced with your life. Take as much time as you need to do this.

Be ready to share a personal story of trust when someone asks you how they will get through their impossible situation.

God will use your story to encourage others and shine the light of Christ.

JOHN 7   (Readings 79–86)

LISTEN
John 7:1–5

¹ After this, Jesus went around in Galilee. He did not want to go about in Judea because the Jewish leaders there were looking for a way to kill him. ² But when the Jewish Festival of Tabernacles was near, ³ Jesus' brothers said to him, "Leave Galilee and go to Judea, so that your disciples there may see the works you do. ⁴ No one who wants to become a public figure acts in secret. Since you are doing these things, show yourself to the world." ⁵ For even his own brothers did not believe in him.

Hear my voice. When you do good, do it behind closed doors.

When you give, do so without any chance to be repaid. When you encourage, do so in private, where the only honor is given to the person you're encouraging.

When you lead, do so with servitude, leading subtly and subversively.

In your work for my kingdom, work in such a way that the glory always goes to me.

Lead people to me, so that they follow my way and not yours.

Give out of my generosity and encourage out of my encouragement.

What is done in secret can have a global impact. Do not underestimate my ability to expand your obedience into a giant harvest.

The farmer works and toils, but the farmer does not get the credit for his crops. No, the crops are a result of my creation process at work. In the same way, participate in my work among people.

Work diligently as for me and not for those around you.

For it is my desire that all should know me, see my glory and respond to those who participate in my work around the world.

What do you hear?

LIVE

How will you respond?

A prompt for living

Throughout your day do secret acts of kindness: Pay someone's toll behind you, pay for the person behind you at the drive-thru, mail an anonymous gift to a friend in need or to a non-profit, drop off gift cards (for a grocery store) to a friend or acquaintance in need, write out your prayers for friends and put them in the mail without your name or a return address.

There are so many ideas.

Choose something and do it! Shhhh . . . it's a secret!

LISTEN
John 7:6-9

⁶ Therefore Jesus told them, "My time is not yet here; for you any time will do. ⁷ The world cannot hate you, but it hates me because I testify that its works are evil. ⁸ You go to the festival. I am not going up to this festival, because my time has not yet fully come." ⁹ After he had said this, he stayed in Galilee.

Reading

80

The days are evil. The world is full of evil. It permeates culture and is often celebrated as entertainment.

Evil comes in many forms. It entices as it draws people in. Evil is present.

You do not like to think of evil. You do not like to recognize that it is here and that at times you celebrate it and other times you participate in it.

Evil is here.

I call out the evil I see. I do not with hold my tongue. You wince at the thought.

You prefer to blame evil on inanimate and soulless objects. You prefer to blame your circumstance, your enemies, and even your friends.

You do not own the fact that evil exists and that at times you play with it.

It is part of the great evil one's plan. He does not want you to believe in evil. He does not want you to believe that you are capable of even an evil thought. This is a lie and it will do you no good.

It may feel good for your pride but it will crush you and keep you distant from me.

I want you to believe that I am good.

I long for you to trust me over the voice of the enemy.

My desire is that you renounce evil and keep far from its influence.

Confess that you are drawn to things that are evil and this will actually draw you into deeper relationship with me; for it shows your ultimate trust in my character and way.

Yes, evil is present, but I am the great victor and when you abide in me, you also experience victory over evil.

Lean into me, trust me, share with me, and turn to me for I am good and desire only good for you.

What do you hear?

LIVE

How will
you respond?

A prompt
for living

When you encounter evil, pray that God will protect you.
Confess that there is evil around you and turn in the opposite direction.

When you see an individual in your life be tempted with evil, pray for them.
Then invite them to something good. Give another option to the evil alluring them in.
Be light!

LISTEN
John 7:10-13

¹⁰ However, after his brothers had left for the festival, he went also, not publicly, but in secret. ¹¹ Now at the festival the Jewish leaders were watching for Jesus and asking, "Where is he?"¹² Among the crowds there was widespread whispering about him. Some said, "He is a good man." Others replied, "No, he deceives the people." ¹³ But no one would say anything publicly about him for fear of the leaders.

What you think of my Son is crucial. Every person who hears of him, has a response to him. You too have an opinion about him.

There are times you treat him as though he was simply a good man.

What do you hear?

There are also times when you question if he truly is my Son who creates a way for you to have relationship with me.

There are times where you do not speak of him, for you fear the opinion of others more than you fear me.

READING
81

Dear child, my longing is for you to believe that Jesus is my Son, that he came to earth living among his creation, and he came because of my great love for you and to build a bridge to me.

LIVE

I continue to be timely in revealing the deep and life-changing truths of my Son.

I hear your prayers and cries for those who do not believe. Continue to pray. I am at work.

How will you respond?

I will increase your faith as I await the exact time to awaken individuals to the truth of Jesus.

Believe. Be at peace. Love others. Speak my name. By this you affirm the truth of Jesus and worship me in spirit and in truth.

A prompt for living

Sit in silence and ask Jesus if there is a country or people group who He desires for you to pray for today. When a country or people group come to mind, pray that the people who fill land or make up the group would know the name of Jesus and that they would receive His love for them.

LISTEN
John 7:14-18

14 Not until halfway through the festival did Jesus go up to the temple courts and begin to teach. 15 The Jews there were amazed and asked, "How did this man get such learning without having been taught?" 16 Jesus answered, "My teaching is not my own. It comes from the one who sent me. 17 Anyone who chooses to do the will of God will find out whether my teaching comes from God or whether I speak on my own. 18 Whoever speaks on their own does so to gain personal glory, but he who seeks the glory of the one who sent him is a man of truth; there is nothing false about him.

When my word is spoken the result will always be the same. Amazement.

My truth is incredibly rich and because I spoke life into existence, my truth resonates deeply within you. When my words are spoken you will be amazed.

You will have a response. For all people, everywhere respond in some way to my word.

Some are amazed and turn away from my words out of fear or because the enemy has so convinced them that the lies he sells are true, that my word seems foolish. When my Spirit is not in someone, my words do not resonate within, for life has not yet over taken them.

You however, have been amazed at my teaching and have chosen to turn to me and trust me.

My words are the very words of life. My son is the word of life made flesh. Life is His name.

My Holy Spirit is life that is given to you as you believe my word, when you believe in me. You feel him deep inside of you when my word is spoken, for he has taken up residence within you and he resonates with that which is true.

You can know when words are spoken from false motive or manipulation for my Holy Spirit will fight against them. My Holy Spirit, My Son, and I are together one, working in you, teaching you, guiding you, and revealing that which is good, right, and perfect.

Listen carefully my child. Let my words be your only source of life.

What do you hear?

LIVE

How will you respond?

A prompt for living

Do you know someone who speaks curses and lies over others? Maybe someone who has spoken lies over you?

Take time right now to pray for them. Pray that God whose word is true, would bless this person with His truth and reveal His glory to him or her.

READING
82

LISTEN
John 7:18-24

[18] Whoever speaks on their own does so to gain personal glory, but he who seeks the glory of the one who sent him is a man of truth; there is nothing false about him. [19] Has not Moses given you the law? Yet not one of you keeps the law. Why are you trying to kill me?"[20] "You are demon-possessed," the crowd answered. "Who is trying to kill you?" [21] Jesus said to them, "I did one miracle, and you are all amazed. [22] Yet, because Moses gave you circumcision (though actually it did not come from Moses, but from the patriarchs), you circumcise a boy on the Sabbath. [23] Now if a boy can be circumcised on the Sabbath so that the law of Moses may not be broken, why are you angry with me for healing a man's whole body on the Sabbath? 24 Stop judging by mere appearances, but instead judge correctly."

READING

83

You have created a law of your own. You have made judgments about what should and shouldn't be. You've chosen to interpret my words in a way that create boxes of safety to keep people in and out.

You have turned good into law and use it to judge others.

Mere appearances mean little. It is not the appearance that matters, for man can staple fruit on a tree, but that does not mean fruit has actually grown. You can put on behaviors and look the part and still remain distant from me.

The heart is what matters. Trust me in this. Trust that your love for and trust in me is what matters.

Seek first me and my kingdom and I will grow in you. I will give you a heart of compassion for others. I will grow in you what is good. Your life will grow fruit. It will be fruit that lasts.

Trust that I too am God of others. Allow me to be the judge. Allow me to be the ultimate authority. Pray for, serve, ask questions, encourage, and speak the truth that I am good and that I desire good for all people. Point people to me and allow me to be the one who convicts.

I do grow fruit in the lives of those who abide in me. When your life or the life of those around you does not reflect the fruit of my Spirit, instead of making judgments come to me, bring others to me in prayer and ask to remove any hindrance of abiding.

What do you hear?

LIVE

How will
you respond?

A prompt
for living

Is there a person in your life you have judged based upon their life choices?

Maybe a religious elite person, a person who belongs to a church you judge, someone who is gay, someone who is struggling with addiction, someone who talks poorly of others or who is consumeristic.

Pray for a soft heart and right spirit towards them. Ask God to give you a heart of generosity, honesty, and grace for this person. Ask God to deepen your own root system as you pray that God will draw this person into a deeper abiding.

Respond with action to any prompting Holy Spirit gives you as you pray.

LISTEN
John 7:25-35

²⁵ At that point some of the people of Jerusalem began to ask, "Isn't this the man they are trying to kill? ²⁶ Here he is, speaking publicly, and they are not saying a word to him. Have the authorities really concluded that he is the Messiah? ²⁷ But we know where this man is from; when the Messiah comes, no one will know where he is from." ²⁸ Then Jesus, still teaching in the temple courts, cried out, "Yes, you know me, and you know where I am from. I am not here on my own authority, but he who sent me is true. You do not know him, ²⁹ but I know him because I am from him and he sent me." 30 At this they tried to seize him, but no one laid a hand on him, because his hour had not yet come. ³¹ Still, many in the crowd believed in him. They said, "When the Messiah comes, will he perform more signs than this man?" ³² The Pharisees heard the crowd whispering such things about him. Then the chief priests and the Pharisees sent temple guards to arrest him. ³³ Jesus said, "I am with you for only a short time, and then I am going to the one who sent me. ³⁴ You will look for me, but you will not find me; and where I am, you cannot come." ³⁵ The Jews said to one another, "Where does this man intend to go that we cannot find him? Will he go where our people live scattered among the Greeks, and teach the Greeks? ³⁶ What did he mean when he said, 'You will look for me, but you will not find me,' and 'Where I am, you cannot come'?"

Reading
84

I know what you are thinking. I know the questions you bring to me. They do not surprise me. In fact I expect questions from you.

Your questions are your way of trying to make sense of mystery. They are also your way of putting human logic to work.

But, human logic doesn't work with me.

I am all knowing. I am all powerful. I am in all.
I am above all. I am the beginning and I am the end.

This is who I am.

You are finite.

Your thinking and desires to understand come from a desire to control, to hold the answers, to play my role.

You will never play my role.

Praise me for this.

If you could, I would not be worth your worship.

But my dear child, I am worth your worship. I am at work in mystery. I use all things. I am sovereign and intentional. There are no surprises to me.

This is hard for you to understand, for human logic sees only the world from one angle, not from the outlook of eternity.

I have eternity and every human everywhere in mind as I work. This is much too big for you.

Today I ask you to trust me with your questions. Trust that I know what you are thinking and will answer you with truth. I love you. I long for you to live in my love and trust that the mysteries to you are not lost on me. I hold you in my hands. Do not push me away.

What do
you hear?

LIVE

How will
you respond?

A prompt
for living

Host a dinner party and ask each person to write on a piece of paper one question they'd like answered by God.

Have discussion about the questions.

In the end, ask if you can pray blessing over the people present. Pray that God would bless them in their search for answers and pray that Jesus would be made known in the process, to the glory of God and by His power.

LISTEN
John 7:37-39

37 On the last and greatest day of the festival, Jesus stood and said in a loud voice, "Let anyone who is thirsty come to me and drink. 38 Whoever believes in me, as Scripture has said, rivers of living water will flow from within them." 39 By this he meant the Spirit, whom those who believed in him were later to receive. Up to that time the Spirit had not been given, since Jesus had not yet been glorified.

You have been given a precious gift. This gift is my Spirit, which indwells you and was given when you first believed in my Son.

You often act as though you do not need my Spirit. You believe you are capable of life apart from me. I've given you my Spirit to speak to you. With him you are able to see with my eyes. You can walk through a day and notice me and recognize my invitations to life for you and those around you. My Spirit is a precious and valuable gift.

What do you hear?

READING
85

It is my desire that you trust in my Spirit within you.

He is always at work.

He is a constant presence of hope, life, and faith.

The fruit of His presence within you is love, joy, peace, patience, kindness, goodness, gentleness, and self-control. When you believe in my Son, my Spirit resides within you and these qualities become the qualities of your life.

I long for you to depend on my Spirit, to listen to him, to trust His promptings and to be obedient as he moves and works within you.

You are not alone. You cannot produce my fruit apart from me.

There is so much I have for you and it is my desire that you live into the fullness of relationship with me. Listen to my Spirit. Trust His voice. He will always lead you to life.

LIVE

How will you respond?

A prompt for living

Begin your day with these words: I choose life today. I choose Jesus. I believe He is good and right and perfect. I believe that Holy Spirit desires to work in me and through me.

Lord, help me to see with your eyes, hear with your ears, and respond with your hands.

Live in response to those words.

At the end of each week share your stories of how Holy Spirit worked through you with a friend or group of friends. Celebrate together!

⁴⁰ On hearing his words, some of the people said, "Surely this man is the Prophet." ⁴¹ Others said, "He is the Messiah." Still others asked, "How can the Messiah come from Galilee? ⁴² Does not Scripture say that the Messiah will come from David's descendants and from Bethlehem, the town where David lived?" ⁴³ Thus the people were divided because of Jesus. ⁴⁴ Some wanted to seize him, but no one laid a hand on him. ⁴⁵ Finally the temple guards went back to the chief priests and the Pharisees, who asked them, "Why didn't you bring him in?" ⁴⁶ "No one ever spoke the way this man does," the guards replied. ⁴⁷ "You mean he has deceived you also?" the Pharisees retorted. ⁴⁸ "Have any of the rulers or of the Pharisees believed in him? ⁴⁹ No! But this mob that knows nothing of the law—there is a curse on them." ⁵⁰ Nicodemus, who had gone to Jesus earlier and who was one of their own number, asked, ⁵¹ "Does our law condemn a man without first hearing him to find out what he has been doing?" ⁵² They replied, "Are you from Galilee, too? Look into it, and you will find that a prophet does not come out of Galilee." ⁵³ Then they all went home.

I know that you have questions. Am I who I say I am? Am I good? Am I for you? Am I right? Am I perfect? I know the questions of your heart.

I know these questions are also the questions you bring to my Son. Is Jesus who he says he is? Is he good? Is he for me?

I am not afraid of your questions. In fact, I love them. I place questions in you that I intend to answer.

It is my desire that you bring your questions to me.

Search me out and I will reveal to you the truth.

Trust and obedience is your response to this truth.

Today, as you come up against difficult situations, bring your questions to me.

When you are worried, bring it to me.

When you are burdened and think I've left you, bring this fear and load to me.

I am who I am—I am good—I am for you.

Your questions will lead you to me, when you bring them to me.

What do you hear?

LIVE

How will you respond?

A prompt for living

Invite a group of friends over for dinner. Have every person write down the questions they have about God, Jesus, or Holy Spirit on slips of paper. Put the questions in a hat, bowl, or whatever and draw out a question to discuss that night at dinner.

Ask if the group would want to keep getting together once a week for dinner until each question has been discussed.

Enjoy!

JOHN 8 (Readings 87–92)

¹ but Jesus went to the Mount of Olives ² At dawn he appeared again in the temple courts, where all the people gathered around him, and he sat down to teach them. ³ The teachers of the law and the Pharisees brought in a woman caught in adultery. They made her stand before the group ⁴ and said to Jesus, "Teacher, this woman was caught in the act of adultery. ⁵ In the Law Moses commanded us to stone such women. Now what do you say?" ⁶ They were using this question as a trap, in order to have a basis for accusing him. But Jesus bent down and started to write on the ground with his finger. ⁷ When they kept on questioning him, he straightened up and said to them, "Let any one of you who is without sin be the first to throw a stone at her." ⁸ Again he stooped down and wrote on the ground. ⁹ At this, those who heard began to go away one at a time, the older ones first, until only Jesus was left, with the woman still standing there. ¹⁰ Jesus straightened up and asked her, "Woman, where are they? Has no one condemned you?" ¹¹ "No one, sir," she said. "Then neither do I condemn you," Jesus declared. "Go now and leave your life of sin."

READING

87

There is condemnation all around you. The world condemns. Those in my church condemn. You have an enemy who constantly is condemning you.

My beautiful child. I see your life. I know your heart. I am in tune with the fact that there is much in this world seeking to kill, steal, and destroy you. These come from the enemy of life, a voice constantly speaking lies over those I love.

I am not that voice.

I am not the voice of shame you hear.

I am not the overwhelming guilt you feel.

I am not the one who takes pleasure in failures and pain.

I am not full of condemnation.

Do not mistake my voice for such things!

There is no condemnation for those found in my Son.

He has written a message of love for you and he stands with you. He stands with you when those around you see your failures. When your deepest secrets are unveiled, he's not surprised by your story.

He stands with you, reminding you of His great love for you, pointing you toward me and inviting you to a better way.

Take His invitation to leave the sin that so easily entangles you. Leave the sin that is coupled with condemnation from the enemy of life and walk in the life my Son offers. For this life is unparalleled.

What do you hear?

LIVE

How will
you respond?

A prompt
for living

Who do you condemn?

What name or people group instantly came to mind?

Make a mental note.

Pray that God will give you compassion, grace, and love for this person or group of people.

Do something this week to love, show compassion, extend grace, or value this person or group.

Depend on Jesus to do this through you, for this kind of love can only come from Jesus, in whom you abide!

LISTEN
John 8:12

12 When Jesus spoke again to the people, he said, "I am the light of the world. Whoever follows me will never walk in darkness, but will have the light of life."

Dear child. I know that in your life you experience much darkness. I know that you walk through periods of time where it feels as though darkness surrounds you and it encroaches on your life.

I know that you experience fear, doubt, grief, dismay, and you long for light.

Your longing for light is a longing for me.

I have placed in you this longing for my life-giving light.

As you walk with my Son, my light in the world, you will know light, even when you are surrounded by darkness. Though at times the darkness seems to encroach on your light, you can be confident that this light, the light of my Son, will never leave you.

Therefore, when trouble comes, remember that the darkness is as light to me. Remember that in me there is no darkness at all. Remember that I am good, and always desire good for my children. With these words, enter the darkness without fear, doubt, grief, or dismay. Enter the darkness with hope, that these momentary troubles will soon pass and you will once again feel the warmth of my light.

Reading
88

What do you hear?

LIVE

How will you respond?

A prompt for living

Keep a candle light in your house at all times. Or, put electric candles in your front windows, lighting them every evening.

When someone asks about your candle or the lights in the windows, take a moment to tell them how these lights are a reminder that even in the darkness there is hope in Jesus, the light of the world.

LISTEN
John 8:13-20

13 The Pharisees challenged him, "Here you are, appearing as your own witness; your testimony is not valid." 14 Jesus answered, "Even if I testify on my own behalf, my testimony is valid, for I know where I came from and where I am going. But you have no idea where I come from or where I am going. 15 You judge by human standards; I pass judgment on no one. 16 But if I do judge, my decisions are true, because I am not alone. I stand with the Father, who sent me. 17 In your own Law it is written that the testimony of two witnesses is true. 18 I am one who testifies for myself; my other witness is the Father, who sent me." 19 Then they asked him, "Where is your father?" "You do not know me or my Father," Jesus replied. "If you knew me, you would know my Father also." 20 He spoke these words while teaching in the temple courts near the place where the offerings were put. Yet no one seized him, because his hour had not yet come.

My grace is sufficient for you. I love you dearly. I want you to know my great love for you. My love for you is evidenced in my Son. When you learn of my Son, you learn of me, for I stand with him. He is the very representation of me.

My son was light, is light.

He illumines the darkness and is not overcome by any evil. My son speaks life over people and invites them to a better way.

My son is good and right and perfect in all His teaching and all of His ways.

I stand with my Son. I am Light. I am Love. I am Truth. I am Grace. I am Provision. I am Hope. I am Joy. I am that I am.

My son is a perfect reflection of me.

Be encouraged today. The truth of my character is revealed through the life of my Son.

You may have hope and life and light. You may have truth and provision and joy. You have the Great I am as you place yourself in the care of my Son, when you entrust your life to me.

What do you hear?

LIVE

How will you respond?

A prompt for living

We each have friends who know us well. People who can vouch for us and affirm the character we posses.

When we choose to invest in a person it is important to learn of their friends and to meet them.

Write a card, Facebook message, text, or email to a close friend of a friend. Do this to encourage this person. Let them know what you know of them because of your friend. It will be a great surprise and will encourage two people at one time. (your friend and your friend's friend)

²¹ Once more Jesus said to them, "I am going away, and you will look for me, and you will die in your sin. Where I go, you cannot come." ²² This made the Jews ask, "Will he kill himself? Is that why he says, 'Where I go, you cannot come'?" ²³ But he continued, "You are from below; I am from above. You are of this world; I am not of this world. ²⁴ I told you that you would die in your sins; if you do not believe that I am he, you will indeed die in your sins." ²⁵ "Who are you?" they asked. "Just what I have been telling you from the beginning," Jesus replied. ²⁶ "I have much to say in judgment of you. But he who sent me is trustworthy, and what I have heard from him I tell the world." ²⁷ They did not understand that he was telling them about his Father. ²⁸ So Jesus said, "When you have lifted up the Son of Man, then you will know that I am he and that I do nothing on my own but speak just what the Father has taught me. ²⁹ The one who sent me is with me; he has not left me alone, for I always do what pleases him." ³¹ To the Jews who had believed him, Jesus said, "If you hold to my teaching, you are really my disciples. ³² Then you will know the truth, and the truth will set you free."

Reading

90

There are many ties that bind you: lies you heard as a child, words spoken over you which formed you, and events that secured an idea, belief or thought. These at times were words of truth, but all too often these were words of death, words that killed, and destroyed.

These ties have kept you bound for years.

I weep with you over these beliefs.

When a word fills you with shame, it is not from me.

When a thought causes you to believe you'll be loved if or when . . . you can know for certain those ideas are not mine.

Truth always brings freedom.

I long for you to know freedom.

I weep over your captivity.

I mourn over your belief that I will love you more if you do this or that.

When these words are spoken as though they are from me, I am filled with anger over the injustice. When those who shepherd, parent, or influence speak words of shame, condemnation, and condition over you, I grieve.

I know the world in which you live loves to believe and live into lies of the enemy; this is one of the reasons I sent my Son. He came to set the captive free. He came to speak life. He came to take the pain of your beating. He came to feel the wound of the lie and place truth over you.

Believe the truth. Truth will always, always, ALWAYS, breathe life. It will always produce fruit. It will always heal. It will always lead to life. It will always point to my great and abundant love for you.

Oh sweet child. My love for you is great.

Put on truth.

Believe what is good and right and perfect.

Live into the reality that in my Son, there is no condemnation, there is no guilt or shame, there is not condition, there is no if only, there is only grace, mercy, and love.

What do
you hear?

LIVE

How will
you respond?

A prompt
for living

Write five cards to five people that simply speak truth over them. Choose people at work, neighbors, your spouse, a long lost friend, or any other person. Choose those who don't know Jesus and those who do. Pray that God would give you words of life for them and write in response to these promptings.

Speak life! Speak truth! Speak freedom!

33 They answered him, "We are Abraham's descendants and have never been slaves of anyone. How can you say that we shall be set free?" 34 Jesus replied, "Very truly I tell you, everyone who sins is a slave to sin. 35 Now a slave has no permanent place in the family, but a son belongs to it forever. 36 So if the Son sets you free, you will be free indeed. 37 I know that you are Abraham's descendants. Yet you are looking for a way to kill me, because you have no room for my word. 38 I am telling you what I have seen in the Father's presence, and you are doing what you have heard from your father." 39 "Abraham is our father," they answered. "If you were Abraham's children," said Jesus, "then you would do what Abraham did. 40 As it is, you are looking for a way to kill me, a man who has told you the truth that I heard from God. Abraham did not do such things. 41 You are doing the works of your own father." "We are not illegitimate children," they protested. "The only Father we have is God himself." 42 Jesus said to them, "If God were your Father, you would love me, for I have come here from God. I have not come on my own; God sent me. 43 Why is my language not clear to you? Because you are unable to hear what I say. 44 You belong to your father, the devil, and you want to carry out your father's desires. He was a murderer from the beginning, not holding to the truth, for there is no truth in him. When he lies, he speaks his native language, for he is a liar and the father of lies. 45 Yet because I tell the truth, you do not believe me! 46 Can any of you prove me guilty of sin? If I am telling the truth, why don't you believe me? 47 Whoever belongs to God hears what God says. The reason you do not hear is that you do not belong to God."

The enemy of truth is at work. He constantly puts ideas before you to believe. Ideas and thoughts about yourself, about my word . . . about me.

His entire objective is to destroy life.

It is easy for you to believe what he says, for his voice has been loud in your life from the beginning.

Be cautious when you take in ideas and make agreements with them.

I am Life. In me there is no death. I speak only words of truth. When I speak, it is often difficult for you to believe my words. At times this is because the words seem too good to be true. Other times it is because you've listened to the father of lies for far too long.

When you know me, you know life, and my words become your source of life.

When my words are hard to believe or even recognize spend time with me.

When you know me, you will be able to recognize me. Truth is always coupled with love and truth always leads towards life.

When you know me, the very giver of life, you are able to recognize my words for they will lead you to life, they will lead you to me.

Listen my beloved. I speak these words because I love you. Come to me, spend time with me, get to know me, and I will bring you life.

What do
you hear?

LIVE

How will
you respond?

A prompt
for living

Listen for lies when others talk around you. When you hear someone self-deprecate, make plans based on fear, or speak words that destroy about self or others, pray instantly that God would give you words of life for this person.

Speak truth into this person.

Speak, write a card, send an email, whatever best fits the situation, but communicate truth to this person, truth that leads towards life.

LISTEN
John 8:48-59

⁴⁸ The Jews answered him, "Aren't we right in saying that you are a Samaritan and demon-possessed?" ⁴⁹ "I am not possessed by a demon," said Jesus, "but I honor my Father and you dishonor me. ⁵⁰ I am not seeking glory for myself; but there is one who seeks it, and he is the judge. ⁵¹ Very truly I tell you, whoever obeys my word will never see death." ⁵² At this they exclaimed, "Now we know that you are demon-possessed! Abraham died and so did the prophets, yet you say that whoever obeys your word will never taste death. ⁵³ Are you greater than our father Abraham? He died, and so did the prophets. Who do you think you are?" ⁵⁴ Jesus replied, "If I glorify myself, my glory means nothing. My Father, whom you claim as your God, is the one who glorifies me. 55 Though you do not know him, I know him. If I said I did not, I would be a liar like you, but I do know him and obey his word. 56 Your father Abraham rejoiced at the thought of seeing my day; he saw it and was glad." 57 "You are not yet fifty years old," they said to him, "and you have seen Abraham!" 58 "Very truly I tell you," Jesus answered, "before Abraham was born, I am!" 59 At this, they picked up stones to stone him, but Jesus hid himself, slipping away from the temple grounds.

It is true that I am, that I am.

At times you accept and at times you fight this truth.

It seems easier to believe in yourself, a friend, your pastor, a mentor, your community, and even strangers. When you place your well-being and hope in the hands of men, they will fail you.

I am hope.

I am life.

I am truth.

I am grace.

I am peace.

I am safety.

I am love.

I am security.

I am faithful.

I am by nature good and right and perfect.

May your hope be put in nothing less,

When you wonder who is with you; remember, I am.

When you question your source of hope; remember, I am.

When you need provision and look for it in many things; remember; I am.

When trials come and you cry out for help; remember, I am.

When you are sick and in need of healing, you ask who will be my healer. Remember, I am.

When the task seems daunting and you cannot accomplish it on your own. You ask who will be your help. Remember, I am.

When the decision is confusing, you ask who will be my truth. Remember, I am.

I am.

What do
you hear?

LIVE

How will
you respond?

A prompt
for living

Is there a place in a friend's life where they are placing their hope in something other than I AM?

Give a small gift and write a card with a word of encouragement that speaks to the fact of sure hope in the person of Jesus.

JOHN 9   (Readings 93–99)

LISTEN
John 9:1-3

¹ As he went along, he saw a man blind from birth. ² His disciples asked him, "Rabbi, who sinned, this man or his parents, that he was born blind?" ³ "Neither this man nor his parents sinned," said Jesus, "but this happened so that the works of God might be displayed in him.

You are a display of my glory.

Every situation in your life is an opportunity for me to reveal the works of my kingdom and my way.

I bring life and light to all things.

This light and life isn't always in the form of physical healing, there are times when the life goes beyond your body.

My glory displayed is found in freedom from shame, oppression, anger, ties that bind you, and the heaviness that you carry.

My glory revealed is found in provision for your health, your physical needs, your daily bread, words of wisdom, insight, encouragement, and hope.

My glory shown is found in healing from heartache, grief, loneliness, injury, illness, hurt, and sin.

My glory is painted on the canvas of your life through sight: When you are able to see a greater plan, when you're able to see truth, when you are able to see beauty, when you able to see a person over an issue, when you are able to see through eyes of grace, when you are able to see the forgotten, when you are able to see good.

My glory is beautiful and it comes in many forms displayed on the lives of those I love.

What do you hear?

LIVE

How will you respond?

A prompt for living

Take a field trip with a friend going through a rough time in life. Go for a hike, camping, a walk, to a museum, or even a stroll downtown in your city.

As you walk, point out any place where you see the glory of God.

Sight gives birth to sight . . . as you point out the glory of God on display, in natural conversation, you are encouraging your friend to see outside of his current circumstance.

LISTEN
John 9:4-7

⁴ As long as it is day, we must do the works of him who sent me. Night is coming, when no one can work. ⁵ While I am in the world, I am the light of the world." ⁶ After saying this, he spit on the ground, made some mud with the saliva, and put it on the man's eyes. ⁷ "Go," he told him, "wash in the Pool of Siloam" (this word means "Sent"). So the man went and washed, and came home seeing.

My dear beloved, I see you.

I see you pray and long for answers.

You long for loved ones to know me.

You long for wisdom about a life situation.

You grieve over loss.

You need instant provision.

You carry the weight of heavy burdens and you are not walking in my light.

I hear your prayers.

I am in the process of answering each and every one of them.

I know it feels like I've simply made things muddier and messier than they were when you came to me. Instead of a one-time answer, and poof! All your troubles go away, I make mud and cover your requests.

I make mud.

It is yours to wash away the mud and realize that the answers have come. I make mud as an invitation to trust. I make mud to send you out. I make mud to reveal my glory. I make mud so you become a participant.

It is mine to heal. It is mine to restore. It is mine to provide. It is mine to bring light and it is mine to lift burdens. Your participation comes as you wash the mud from your eyes, as you clean away the muck believing that when the mud is lifted, you will see!

When you are invited to participate in an answer to prayer, do not balk at it, seek me, believe, go out, participate, wash, and walk in the answer unveiled.

What do you hear?

LIVE

How will you respond?

A prompt for living

Find a friend to pray with about a given situation. Commit to praying until the prayer is answered. (This may take years!)

Encourage one another as you watch God move, as the situation gets worse before it gets better, as you struggle to believe and finally to celebrate the answer in whatever form it comes.

Prayer will always lead to increased belief!

⁸ His neighbors and those who had formerly seen him begging asked, "Isn't this the same man who used to sit and beg?" ⁹ Some claimed that he was. Others said, "No, he only looks like him."

But he himself insisted, "I am the man." ¹⁰ "How then were your eyes opened?" they asked.

¹¹ He replied, "The man they call Jesus made some mud and put it on my eyes. He told me to go to Siloam and wash. So I went and washed, and then I could see." ¹² "Where is this man?" they asked him. "I don't know," he said.

I have changed you.

I have taken up residence in your heart and you embody me.

I change you.

So much so, that there will be those who will no longer recognize you. They will ask, "Is that really you?" And you will get to answer with a resounding "Yes! It is me! But I am a new creation. The old has gone and the new has come. I am no longer what I used to be."

When I heal you from the inside out, others will take notice. Others will wonder. Others will ask.

Changed lives always lead to inquiry about the change.

When those around you inquire about the change in you, speak of me.

Tell of my faithfulness.

Share of my goodness.

Smile simply and explain the whole thing.

You at once were blind, but now can see.

You were once captive and now you are free.

You were sick and I made you well.

You were heavy burdened and now, you are light.

I have changed you and it is so good.

What do you hear?

LIVE

How will you respond?

A prompt for living

Have you noticed a change in a friend, co-worker, or acquaintance? Speak to the change and ask what was the catalyst.

READING

95

LISTEN
John 9:13-16

[13] They brought to the Pharisees the man who had been blind. [14] Now the day on which Jesus had made the mud and opened the man's eyes was a Sabbath. [15] Therefore the Pharisees also asked him how he had received his sight. "He put mud on my eyes," the man replied, "and I washed, and now I see." [16] Some of the Pharisees said, "This man is not from God, for he does not keep the Sabbath."

In life, you find what it is you are looking for. You discover that which you are disciplined to see. You have trained your senses to notice things through a particular point of view and search for evidence to support it.

All too often you look for me by following a trail made of human ideals. You recognize the idea of me in others as they follow a nice set of rules, look a part, or don't mess with a specific religious system. Rules do not lead to knowledge or intimacy.

You also look for me in human comfort and ease in life. Trials come and go and you wonder where I've gone, because you've only learned to look for me in your own personal comfort.

You miss me because you are not looking for me. No, you look for an idea of me made by man.

Instead consider for a moment the attributes of my character: I am love. I am good. I am truth. I am faithful. I am gracious. I am just. I am healer.

Every day you encounter even the smallest good.

Many days you know love.

You hear truth and experience it.

You know faithfulness in some form.

At times you are extended grace.

You desire justice.

And, you see my healing in small and large ways.

Every day there are glimpses of my character around you. Look for me!

When you look for me you will find me. This is a promise.

What do you hear?

LIVE

How will you respond?

A prompt for living

Host a dinner party, choose one attribute of God's character. Over the meal ask how each person has experienced that attribute within the last week.

(i.e. if you choose good, ask people how they've experienced good in the past week)

Follow the conversation up with a brief recognition of the fact that this is a character trait of God who is always at work around us. Give thanks and encourage people to keep looking.

Reading

96

¹⁷ Then they turned again to the blind man, "What have you to say about him? It was your eyes he opened." The man replied, "He is a prophet." ¹⁸ They still did not believe that he had been blind and had received his sight until they sent for the man's parents. ¹⁹ "Is this your son?" they asked. "Is this the one you say was born blind? How is it that now he can see?" ²⁰ "We know he is our son," the parents answered, "and we know he was born blind. ²¹ But how he can see now, or who opened his eyes, we don't know. Ask him. He is of age; he will speak for himself." ²² His parents said this because they were afraid of the Jewish leaders, who already had decided that anyone who acknowledged that Jesus was the Messiah would be put out of the synagogue. ²³ That was why his parents said, "He is of age; ask him." ²⁴ A second time they summoned the man who had been blind. "Give glory to God by telling the truth," they said. "We know this man is a sinner." ²⁵ He replied, "Whether he is a sinner or not, I don't know. One thing I do know. I was blind but now I see!"

You were blind and now you see, that is all you need to know. I am the source of your sight. This fact confuses people who look to the things of the world to bring about change.

You were blind. You lived in darkness. But now, oh now my child you see. You live in light.

Believe this. Live in it. It is your reality. It is the very truth of your story. Let this be your hope. When trouble comes, remember when I was your help.

When the air is thick with sadness, remember when I healed you.

When life is full of pain, remember when I gave you joy.

When the attacks seem to come from every side, remember when I protected you.

When the lies seem more believable than the truth, remember when I spoke life over you.

When the darkness seems too dark and the darkness fills the day, remember darkness is as light to me. I am the light of the world. I AM. I bring light and hope and sight to all who trust in me.

Believe in me. Trust me. Bring your darkness to me and I, the maker of heaven and earth, I the light of the world, will give you sight!

What do you hear?

LIVE

How will you respond?

A prompt for living

Do you know someone going through a difficult time? Invite them out for some time with you and extend the hope of Jesus, by listening to, praying with, and trusting for them.

READING
97

LISTEN
John 9:26-34

26 Then they (The Pharisees) asked him, "What did he do to you? How did he open your eyes?"

27 He answered, "I have told you already and you did not listen. Why do you want to hear it again? Do you want to become his disciples too?" 28 Then they hurled insults at him and said, "You are this fellow's disciple! We are disciples of Moses! 29 We know that God spoke to Moses, but as for this fellow, we don't even know where he comes from." 30 The man answered, "Now that is remarkable! You don't know where he comes from, yet he opened my eyes. 31 We know that God does not listen to sinners. He listens to the godly person who does his will. 32 Nobody has ever heard of opening the eyes of a man born blind. 33 If this man were not from God, he could do nothing." 34 To this they replied, "You were steeped in sin at birth; how dare you lecture us!" And they threw him out.

Not all people will want to know the truth of your story. Yes, I have changed you and it is good, but to some, the good I bring is a threat.

Do not hold tightly to the opinion of others. When others speak against me, speak the story of my work in your life.

There are those in life who want to listen to no one outside of their opinion or belief system. You cannot convince others to follow me or to believe your story.

It is not yours to convince, it is yours to tell.

Tell your story over and over.

Be not afraid when others come against you.

Do not strain to make them believe.

You cannot make anyone believe.

Just as I gave you sight, I will give others sight. It is yours to pray. It is yours to tell. It is yours to live. It is yours to reveal. When you do these things you participate in the process of my work unfolding in the lives of others.

I promise that I will continue the work.

Believe in me when others will not believe your story.

Believe in me that I will continue the work of salvation.

Believe in me that I will fully reveal in my time.

Believe in me when others point fingers and blame, because of their own shortsightedness.

Believe in me. It is your greatest work.

What do
you hear?

LIVE

How will
you respond?

A prompt
for living

What is the last prayer request you prayed that you saw God answer?

Don't hold the good to yourself, tell a friend. Make a point to invite even those who do not believe in Jesus, to know the process of prayer and trust, so that your story may be an example of God's work in you!

LISTEN
John 9:35-41

35 Jesus heard that they had thrown him out, and when he found him, he said, "Do you believe in the Son of Man?" 36 "Who is he, sir?" the man asked. "Tell me so that I may believe in him."

37 Jesus said, "You have now seen him; in fact, he is the one speaking with you." 38 Then the man said, "Lord, I believe," and he worshiped him. 39 Jesus said, "For judgment I have come into this world, so that the blind will see and those who see will become blind." 40 Some Pharisees who were with him heard him say this and asked, "What? Are we blind too?" 41 Jesus said, "If you were blind, you would not be guilty of sin; but now that you claim you can see, your guilt remains."

When you are cast aside I will pursue you.

When others turn from you because of me,
I will search you out.

When you are abandoned, I am with you.

When others speak poorly of you because of me,
I am your true identity source.

Put your faith in me.

READING
99

I have given you sight.
I have given you sight so that you can see me.

Sight is an invitation to belief.

When I give you sight, I do so that you will believe.

Think of Paul, before I gave him sight, I took his earthly vision. He needed to experience darkness, so that he could recognize true sight.

Sight is a gift from me.
Sight is for you to believe.

When darkness falls on you, ask me for new sight.
I only bring darkness, to reveal light.
The darkness is never dark to me, for I am light.

Your sight has revealed to you the truths of my kingdom. Believe my child.

What do you hear?

LIVE

How will you respond?

A prompt for living

Think of a person who is walking through a period of darkness in his life.

Pray that God will give him new vision with eyes of the kingdom.

As you pray, if God puts something on your heart, to write or speak or do . . . put those thoughts into action!

JOHN 10 (Readings 100–109)

LISTEN
John 10:1-6

1 "Very truly I tell you Pharisees, anyone who does not enter the sheep pen by the gate, but climbs in by some other way, is a thief and a robber. 2 The one who enters by the gate is the shepherd of the sheep. 3 The gatekeeper opens the gate for him, and the sheep listen to his voice. He calls his own sheep by name and leads them out. 4 When he has brought out all his own, he goes on ahead of them, and his sheep follow him because they know his voice. 5 But they will never follow a stranger; in fact, they will run away from him because they do not recognize a stranger's voice." 6 Jesus used this figure of speech, but the Pharisees did not understand what he was telling them.

What do you hear?

Beware my child. There are many who disguise themselves as me or as one who speaks for me. Their words tickle your ears, inviting you to come and follow a way that leaves no room for me.

Their words lead to short cuts. Their words lead to deceptive ideas and lead you away from me.

Beware of these words.

Beware of these invitations.

I am good. I will always lead you in a good way. The way will not always be easy, but it will always be good and it will always lead you towards me.

Listen carefully.

LIVE

How will you respond?

When you get ideas or when people give you advice, weigh their words. Do the words lead towards me and my way or do they lead you away from me?

These questions are important.

I desire good and life for all my children.

I long for you to know the benefit of living into the good of my kingdom. Though the way is not always easy, it will always lead to me.

Trust and follow.

A prompt for living

Is there someone in your life who is asking for advice?

Instead of being quick to give your opinion and thoughts, pause, ask God to give you words, insight, and wisdom.

Secondly, (if the person is a follow of Jesus) ask what they've felt or heard as they've prayed. Give them time to respond.

Lastly, respond not for their ease, but for their good!

LISTEN
John 10:7-9

> [7] Therefore Jesus said again, "Very truly I tell you, I am the gate for the sheep. [8] All who have come before me are thieves and robbers, but the sheep have not listened to them. [9] I am the gate; whoever enters through me will be saved. They will come in and go out, and find pasture.

I am the entry point.

Come to me as your source.

I am the source. If you place your well-being, your identity or your value in any other source you are placing these things in the hands of thieves and robbers.

Only I am for you. I am for your ultimate good. I am for your well-being. I am for your future. I am for your present.

Place your hope, your value, your identity, your past, present, and future, and your well-being in me.

I am the entry point to life.

All who come to me live, because I am life.

The offer is always before you.

Find your place in me.

May I be the source of your life.

Everything else will leave you wanting.

Reading
101

What do you hear?

LIVE

How will you respond?

A prompt for living

Find a local rescue mission or service opportunity and participate by serving for an evening. (or better yet, make a habit of it) In the midst of serving, pray that God will reveal himself as source to those your serve.

LISTEN
John 10:10

¹⁰ The thief comes only to steal and kill and destroy; I have come that they may have life, and have it to the full.

Be on guard! You have an enemy whose greatest desire is to destroy your life, rob you of any joy and kill off any good. His entire existence is geared towards death and he thoroughly enjoys going after those who bear my image.

What do you hear?

He presents lies that look like truth. He speaks words about your value that sound valid. He tempts you with that which will lead you away from me.

He is my enemy. He detests me. He has been inviting people to turn from me from the very beginning.

"Do not trust God! Don't believe He is good and right and perfect. Don't believe that He has good for you! Take matters into your own hands and grab hold while the gettin's good." Eve tragically made an agreement with the enemy of life and she and her love, Adam, experience separation from me for the very first time.

LIVE

You are given daily opportunities to choose to listen to the voice of my enemy, the enemy of life. Be on guard!

How will you respond?

Look and listen for life. My word will always lead you towards life. My instruction is always for your whole good. My way is always life giving and full of my glory. I desire good for you. This is true. I desire life and not just any life, a full, abundant, and good life.

Choose my words. Obey my instruction. Follow my way. You will find life in me and you will walk in my glory.

My love for you is beyond measure!

Trust me in this.

Listen to me. Look for me and choose life!

A prompt for living

Often good is not convenient. It often takes more time and thought.

As you think of someone in your life who is in need of good. Take the time to write her a letter. Write out your prayer or word of encouragement.

Do this good . . . for their good!

LISTEN
John 10:11-15

[11] "I am the good shepherd. The good shepherd lays down his life for the sheep. [12] The hired hand is not the shepherd and does not own the sheep. So when he sees the wolf coming, he abandons the sheep and runs away. Then the wolf attacks the flock and scatters it. [13] The man runs away because he is a hired hand and cares nothing for the sheep. [14] "I am the good shepherd; I know my sheep and my sheep know me- [15] just as the Father knows me and I know the Father-and I lay down my life for the sheep.

Good is not a word that means below great. *Good* is not a quantifier of enjoyment. *Good* is not a word to describe one's feelings.

Good is the absolute embodiment of all that is right, true, pure, lovely, holy, and trustworthy.

There is only one who is good and that is me. I am the only true and pure good in the world.

I am *Good*.

My character and ways will always reflect this.

My way toward you will always be good.

I am for you. I love you. I know you. I know you so intimately that the numbers of your hairs are counted. I love you so deeply that my Son gave his life for you so that you could share in my kingdom life.

My son is the good shepherd.

He knows you. He watches over you. He sent his Spirit to remain with you.

When you walk through circumstances that are challenging, remember I am good, and I am for you.

When you experience pain, cling to my good and know that I am with you.

When you walk through the valley of the shadow of death, do not fear anything, for I am with you. I am good and I am protecting you and giving you footing.

When you experience that which is bad, know that in me you will live in my good.

My dearest one, I am good. I love you and I am for you. Trust in this.

READING
103

What do
you hear?

LIVE

**How will
you respond?**

**A prompt
for living**

Who is a person in your life who is challenging for you?

Ask Jesus to show you good for that person. Every day for the next several weeks pray good over this person. If an idea comes to you of a way to serve this person, do it. If a word of encouragement comes to you for them, write it in a card and send it.

Listen to Jesus as you pray for this individual to experience good and actively participate in being an extension of God's good to him/her.

LISTEN
John 10:16

16 I have other sheep that are not of this sheep pen. I must bring them also. They too will listen to my voice, and there shall be one flock and one shepherd.

I am your Father and my Son is the good shepherd.

My son knows His sheep. His sheep come in all shapes, sizes, religions, countries, and ethnic backgrounds.

His sheep know His voice. Just as He's called them, wherever they are, they hear His voice and know it's familiar tone.

His sheep hear His voice. They know me, for the good shepherd was sent from me.

Often in this world, conditions are put on individuals as to who can and cannot hear the voice of the good shepherd. But He alone determines to whom He will speak and opens the ears of the hearer. The good shepherd is intimately aware of His sheep. They come from places similar to you and places vastly different.

It is my desire that all sheep become one. Therefore, pay attention to my Spirit and my voice at work with in you.

Listen to me when you hear the stories of those different than you. Do you hear my truth being spoken?
Does my Spirit show you that He resides with someone?

As you walk this journey through life, seek the shepherd. Seek His voice. Listen for Him. Listen to Him. Come to Him when He calls.

Oh my dear child, He is good and His love for you is an exact representation of my love. It is deep and rich and purely good.

Live in this love, extend this love.

Look and listen to those around you so that you may know those who are the good shepherd's sheep around you. Come to me together, love others together, live out the way of the good shepherd together. As you do, you will be known as mine and my glory will be seen in all of the world.

What do you hear?

LIVE

How will you respond?

A prompt for living

Reading
104

Write five cards to local pastors who serve in denominations of which you are not a part. Thank them for their service to the body of Christ and recognize your unity as sheep that follow the good shepherd.

(Just go online look up local churches and write to five pastors. Send the cards to the church address given on the website!)

LISTEN
John 10:17-21

17 The reason my Father loves me is that I lay down my life-only to take it up again. 18 No one takes it from me, but I lay it down of my own accord. I have authority to lay it down and authority to take it up again. This command I received from my Father." 19 The Jews who heard these words were again divided. 20 Many of them said, "He is demon-possessed and raving mad. Why listen to him?" 21 But others said, "These are not the sayings of a man possessed by a demon. Can a demon open the eyes of the blind?"

You seek to understand my words with your mind.

Because I spoke your mind into existence, your mind will not fully understand my ways, for you were my thought before you came to be.

Just as I spoke the world into existence, I breathed life into you and your lungs filled and your soul flourished.

What do you hear?

I know the very details of your mind.

I know the number of cells that make up your brain tissue.

I know every thought. I am aware of every subconscious idea.

LIVE

I am more aware of you than you are.

You are mine. You were made by me.

For this reason, you will never be able to fully understand my ways. My ways are not yours to understand. It is not required of you to understand me. I desire not your understanding, but your belief.

How will you respond?

Understanding is a form of human approval. I do not need the approval of people.

I do however, long for people to believe in me, for it is belief in me that changes everything.

You may not understand my ways, but you can trust them because you believe that I am good.

Is there a situation in life where you do not understand what God is doing?

My ways will always lead to life.

My ways will always be perfect.

Pray that God would use this situation to increase your belief in Him!

A prompt for living

Believe in me! Believe and walk in my ways. Believe in me and walk in truth. Believe in me and walk in life.

Invite a friend to pray with you so that your belief may grow together!

Though you may never understand my ways, believe.

22 Then came the Festival of Dedication at Jerusalem. It was winter, 23 and Jesus was in the temple courts walking in Solomon's Colonnade. 24 The Jews who were there gathered around him, saying, "How long will you keep us in suspense? If you are the Messiah, tell us plainly."

25 Jesus answered, "I did tell you, but you do not believe. The works I do in my Father's name testify about me, 26 but you do not believe because you are not my sheep.

There are many ways to speak plainly. So often you believe you must only use your words to tell my story or speak my truth. But, there are other ways.

Use works in my name to display your belonging.

The works you do in me testify to my work in you. They also testify to my work in the world.

When you do work in my name you display my character for all to see.

You are a lamp on a lamp stand.

You are a city on a hill.

You are my light displayed in the world.

Do not worry about what you should say. I will be your words when you need. But instead, love with your actions. Live generously. Love completely. Don't show any kind of favoritism. Don't hold grudges. Forgive easily. Don't be judgmental. Be kind and patient and thoughtful. Love with the strength you have and I will increase your ability to love as you depend on me.

Do not tell people what righteousness looks like, no, live it.

Do not tell people that I am holy and they are not, no, you believe I am holy and walk in light of my work in your life.

Do not tell people who I am, show them. Let your life be a billboard to my name. Be my ambassador! When you abide in me, you represent me.

Oh my dear child. Let your life point others to me, use words only when necessary.

Reading
106

What do you hear?

LIVE

How will you respond?

A prompt for living

Who is someone in your life you'd like to know Jesus?

Think of one way you can display the love of God to them. Put that idea into practice this week!

LISTEN
John 10:27-30

27 My sheep listen to my voice; I know them, and they follow me. 28 I give them eternal life, and they shall never perish; no one will snatch them out of my hand. 29 My Father, who has given them to me, is greater than all; no one can snatch them out of my Father's hand. 30 I and the Father are one."

My son and I are one. When he holds you, I hold you. When you believe in Him, you believe in me. He is the exact representation of me.

I am life, death does not exist in me. My son is life, he leads people to life. He leads you to life.

He knows those who are his intimately.

He knows the very hairs on your head.

He knows the worries of your heart.

He knows the cares of your mind.

He is intimately aware of your striving and your trust. He knows when you weep and when you are filled with joy.

He knows when you are content and when your heart aches for me.

He knows when you are lonely and when you are full. He knows very intimately your deepest wants and He knows exactly what you need.

He is aware of your every step and you do not leave, even for an instance His watchful care.

He even knows your voice.

Oh my sweet child, you belong to Him, and He will never let you go.

I too will never let you go. I am sovereign. I am holy. I am perfect in every way and I carefully attend to your every care. You will never be snatched from the loving care my Son and I lavish upon you.

Trust this. Live in this. Know the joy that is found in the gift of our love and life for you and in you.

What do you hear?

LIVE

How will you respond?

A prompt for living

Do you know a follower of Jesus who bound by performance?

Take a moment to write some thoughts on the unconditional love of Jesus for them and send it to them in an email, letter, Facebook message, or text.

LISTEN
John 10:31–39

31 Again his Jewish opponents picked up stones to stone him, 32 but Jesus said to them, "I have shown you many good works from the Father. For which of these do you stone me?"

33 "We are not stoning you for any good work," they replied, "but for blasphemy, because you, a mere man, claim to be God." 34 Jesus answered them, "Is it not written in your Law, 'I have said you are "gods"'? 35 If he called them 'gods,' to whom the word of God came-and Scripture cannot be set aside- 36 what about the one whom the Father set apart as his very own and sent into the world? Why then do you accuse me of blasphemy because I said, 'I am God's Son'? 37 Do not believe me unless I do the works of my Father. 38 But if I do them, even though you do not believe me, believe the works, that you may know and understand that the Father is in me, and I in the Father." 39 Again they tried to seize him, but he escaped their grasp.

Reading

108

My works in your life are the greatest evidence you possess that I am who I am.

This is why it is so important that you remember and celebrate. Tell my story to all who will listen. Declare my works to those around you. When I answer prayer, write it down and remember.

When miracles happen, add a stone to the altar of my goodness in your life.

When you collide with unexpected good, take a moment to remember.

Dear child, remembering and telling the stories of me at work in your life are powerful tools. Do not hide the works of my hands under bushels. But let them shine as light, pointing not to your belief, but to My character. I am the object of worship.

I am the one who hears and answers.

I am faithful, true, and good.

Tell my stories. You will bring my name fame and give me glory!

What do you hear?

LIVE

How will you respond?

A prompt for living

What is your last prayer that was answered?

Choose a friend, co-worker, acquaintance, or family member that needs to be encouraged. Share the story of God's faithfulness to you and then ask if you can pray for them right at that moment. Take time to pray right there, wherever you happen to be.

LISTEN
John 10:40-42

⁴⁰ Then Jesus went back across the Jordan to the place where John had been baptizing in the early days. There he stayed, ⁴¹ and many people came to him. They said, "Though John never performed a sign, all that John said about this man was true." ⁴² And in that place many believed in Jesus.

Let your light so shine that others see you and are drawn to my light within.

Light comes as you abide in me and walk in my way.

I do not desire compliance to my way. Compliance is only a legalistic response to a demanding judge.

No, I desire obedience, for it is a response of trust and belief. Obedience comes from within and it is a matter of the heart.

Compliance does not shine light.

But obedience, obedience gives light. When you are obedient to my way, you shine so brightly that others notice instantly.

Abide in me and walk in my way. As you do so, others will see your good deeds and praise me. Live in the freedom of abiding. Live out that freedom through obedience. You will be a road sign pointing others towards me. You will prepare the way for me in the hearts of those with whom your path crosses.

Though you yourself never perform a sign of any kind, let you life speak to the glory of Jesus and may your life point to all his words being true and right and perfect.

READING
109

What do you hear?

LIVE

How will you respond?

A prompt for living

Who are two people in your life whom you trust and with whom you walk?

Bring them together to have a conversation about compliance and obedience. Seek the Lord's wisdom and discernment to see where you are each responding with your life in a compliant way to a judging expector. Also discuss what obedience looks like in your life currently. Pray for each other to live freely in obedience.

John 11 (Readings 110–122)

LISTEN
John 11:1-3

¹ Now a man named Lazarus was sick. He was from Bethany, the village of Mary and her sister Martha. ² (This Mary, whose brother Lazarus now lay sick, was the same one who poured perfume on the Lord and wiped his feet with her hair.) ³ So the sisters sent word to Jesus, "Lord, the one you love is sick."

Be one as my Son and I are one. Relationships are important to me. You were created to live life with others.
You were created to share in experiences of joy and sorrow.
You were not created for independence or isolation.

When you come to me with the pain, sickness, sorrow, and longings of others I first celebrate the love extended. I long for your love of others to drive you to me.

Come to me with desperate pleas for those in your life.
Come to me with praises for my handy work expressed in their lives.

Come to me with their unmet desires.

Come to me with their needs for provision.

Come to me with their heart ache.

Come to me with their illness.

Come to me, trusting that my love for those in your life is more deep and wide and high and long than you could imagine.

My love for those around you will transform your relationships with them. This is also why I ask you to pray for your enemies and those who persecute you. When you pray for your enemies, they become your friends.

Come to me for others, it is a gift to me and a gift to each other.

READING
110

What do you hear?

LIVE

How will you respond?

A prompt for living

Is there a person in your life who challenges you? A political figure? A celebrity? A person at work? Someone who boldly speaks out against that which you love? A relative? A one-time friend?

Make a commitment to pray for this person every day for the next year.
Watch the Lord work through your prayers and increase your capacity to love.

LISTEN
John 11:4

4 When he heard this, Jesus said, "This sickness will not end in death. No, it is for God's glory so that God's Son may be glorified through it."

I watch as you face impossibility after impossibility.
I watch you fear and tremble. I see you struggle for faith.
I know that your situation seems unbearable.

I know your grief, I feel your pain, I cry with you.
None of the reality you walk in is lost on me.

My longing is that you would know the reality of me
in the midst of your circumstance.

I bring death to life.

I bring hope to hopelessness.

I bring restoration to that which is destroyed.

I bring light to darkness.

I bring healing where there is pain.

I bring provision where there is none.

I bring help in your time of trouble.

I bring these things, because I've given you me.

I am life, hope, restoration, light, healing, provision, and help.
Believe in me.

The scope of that which you walk in is grander than you.
It is for me to reveal to a watching world my lavish care and love. I want every person, everywhere, to walk in the reality which I bring. Your life is the main channel to accomplish this.

No part of your story is lost on me, it is all for me and for my purposes. I reveal my glory as you face impossibility. This is a gift for you to increase your faith and to share with the world, so that all may know. Therefore, count it all joy as you face trials of many kinds.

**What do
you hear?**

LIVE

**How will
you respond?**

**A prompt
for living**

Think of a part of the world that seems to be in an impossible situation. Pray that God would reveal himself to those who live in these situations. Pray too that God would make His name famous and that many would come to know Him through his restorative work in the darkest corners of the world.

LISTEN
John 11:5-7

⁵ Now Jesus loved Martha and her sister and Lazarus. ⁶ So when he heard that Lazarus was sick, he stayed where he was two more days, ⁷ and then he said to his disciples, "Let us go back to Judea."

I am sovereign. I am holy. I am right. I am perfect.

In all of my ways. All of the time.

My ways do not make sense to you. When crisis comes you want out. You want to be excused from pain or difficulty. You believe that to experience good you must walk an easy and comfortable road. Ease and comfort are not the definition of good.

Therefore, my love, it is because I love you that you at times suffer. Your pain and difficulty develop in your character, perseverance, and hope.

I do weep with you in your pain and at the same time, rejoice that you are maturing, developing faith and increasing in belief.

Yes, I will deliver you. I will be your rescue. I will come to you. Do not give up hope. My timing is different than yours. I am not cruel. I am always loving. Therefore, I will come to your rescue in my time.

Wait on me. Place your hope in me. And rejoice when the suffering comes and the rescue seems far off. Look to me, hold on to me and believe that I am good and am for yours.

What do you hear?

LIVE

How will you respond?

A prompt for living

Do you know someone going through difficulty?

Make a commitment to pray for them daily. Reach out by writing out your prayers for them and sending them via email or in a card.

Choose to journey with them through darkness, instead of seeking to rescue them out of it prematurely.

LISTEN
John 11:8-10

8 "But Rabbi," they said, "a short while ago the Jews there tried to stone you, and yet you are going back?" 9 Jesus answered, "Are there not twelve hours of daylight? Anyone who walks in the daytime will not stumble, for they see by this world's light. 10 It is when a person walks at night that they stumble, for they have no light."

Sometimes my way brings you into the middle of uncertainty. At times I ask you to walk through the valley of the shadow of death. There are even moments when I invite you to go against logic of this world to obey me.

You see my child, my love for you is so deep and true and good that I invite you to die, so that you may know life. There are many places within you that hold to old ways of thinking and beliefs about me and your own self. I know that dying to these beliefs or stepping into great mystery or going against logic to face the giant will lead you to experience life.

I take you to the valley of the shadow of death, because I know that life in me comes from the death of self.

You can also know that when you walk through the valley of the shadow of death that you need not fear it or any evil you come across along the way, for I am with you. I am both your sure footing and your protection. I am also one who will prepare a table of blessing in the middle of the valley.

Trust in me when I put before you a way that seemingly goes against logic or invites you into the valley. Trust me and step into the valley, for on the other side of the valley is greater intimacy with me and life, abundant, and full.

READING

113

What do you hear?

LIVE

How will you respond?

A prompt for living

Do you know someone who is walking through a valley? Invite them over for a meal and encourage them. Lavish them with generous and unwarranted hospitality. When they ask why, speak to Jesus.

LISTEN
John 11:11-16

11 After he had said this, he went on to tell them, "Our friend Lazarus has fallen asleep; but I am going there to wake him up." 12 His disciples replied, "Lord, if he sleeps, he will get better." 13 Jesus had been speaking of his death, but his disciples thought he meant natural sleep. 14 So then he told them plainly, "Lazarus is dead, 15 and for your sake I am glad I was not there, so that you may believe. But let us go to him." 16 Then Thomas (also known as Didymus) said to the rest of the disciples, "Let us also go, that we may die with him."

I am at work in your life for your sake as well as for the belief of others. Situations arise and you walk through them. The depths and heights to which I take you are a picture of my boundless care, provision, and faithfulness.

I brought the Israelites out of Egypt for their good, but also for your encouragement.

I parted the waters as the enemy pressed in for their safety and for your encouragement to hope.

I gave daily provisions of food to sustain them and to encourage you to believe.

I brought the Israelites into the promise land for their home and to encourage you to trust.

My son was not with Lazarus when he died, so that he could bring life from death; for Lazarus, for the belief of those who watched and for the belief of the many who would hear of the story.

I do the same with you. I work for your good and also for the encouragement of those who hear the stories of your life.

Trust me when you come against impossibility, when you need provision, when you need a home, when you need life. Trust me, walk in my truth, and share the story of my faithfulness to you.

**What do
you hear?**

LIVE

**How will
you respond?**

**A prompt
for living**

Take some time to remember. What good have you experienced of the Lord this past year. Write it down. After you've written your list, call a friend, get together for coffee and share your list with them! Remember and celebrate together.

17 On his arrival, Jesus found that Lazarus had already been in the tomb for four days. 18 Now Bethany was less than two miles from Jerusalem, 19 and many Jews had come to Martha and Mary to comfort them in the loss of their brother. 20 When Martha heard that Jesus was coming, she went out to meet him, but Mary stayed at home. 21 "Lord," Martha said to Jesus, "if you had been here, my brother would not have died. 22 But I know that even now God will give you whatever you ask."

There are times where it feels as though I've failed you. There are times where your prayers are not answered how you think best. There are times when your dreams die, the pain remains, the sickness doesn't go away, the relationship doesn't mend, the money doesn't come, the troubles seemingly get worse. In these times do not think that I have forgotten you. I am neither blind nor negligent. Your loss is seen and felt.

Instead of assuming I've left or blaming me for the reality you want but do not have, run to me. Run to me with your questions. Run to me with your unanswered prayers. Seek me in your anger. Find me, when you don't understand. Look for me in your grief. I am not thrown by these things. Nor do these things anger me. My love for you is deep and I am capable of the impossible, for nothing is impossible with me. Run to me and believe.

READING
115

**What do
you hear?**

LIVE

**How will
you respond?**

**A prompt
for living**

Get a group of friends to put together gift baskets to take to local hospitals. Leave a gift basket with the attendant of the Intensive Care waiting room. Leave a note that although you do not know the extent of the circumstance, that you will be praying for every person in the waiting room that they would know healing, hope, and feel loved.

LISTEN
John 11:23-27

23 Jesus said to her, "Your brother will rise again." 24 Martha answered, "I know he will rise again in the resurrection at the last day." 25 Jesus said to her, "I am the resurrection and the life. The one who believes in me will live, even though they die; 26 and whoever lives by believing in me will never die. Do you believe this?" 27 "Yes, Lord," she replied, "I believe that you are the Messiah, the Son of God, who is to come into the world."

Do you believe this? Do you believe that my Son is the resurrection and the life? When you believe, you live, even when you die. When you live by believing you never die. Life is my name. Life is the way of my Son. Life is his truth. He created life. He founded it and he loves to see you walk in the way of life.

Your answer to this question of belief is crucial. Your life depends on it. You may say you are a Christian, but participating in religious practices does not assume belief.

When you believe in me, when you follow the way of my Son, your life changes. Your belief counts. It makes a difference. It is your life-line.

Your belief is your hardest work.

Work hard to believe in every situation. Actively place your trust in my Son, in me. Do not lean upon your own understanding but in all your ways acknowledge me, believe in my Son and as one, we will direct your path.

What do you hear?

LIVE

How will you respond?

A prompt for living

Do a personal belief inventory. Where is it easy for you to believe? Where is it difficult?

Grab a couple of friends and ask them to do the same. Get together and talk about your belief and unbelief. Pray with each other for increased belief and encourage one another continually to walk in the way of belief in Jesus.

LISTEN
John 11:28-32

28 After she had said this, she went back and called her sister Mary aside. "The Teacher is here," she said, "and is asking for you." 29 When Mary heard this, she got up quickly and went to him. 30 Now Jesus had not yet entered the village, but was still at the place where Martha had met him. 31 When the Jews who had been with Mary in the house, comforting her, noticed how quickly she got up and went out, they followed her, supposing she was going to the tomb to mourn there. 32 When Mary reached the place where Jesus was and saw him, she fell at his feet and said, "Lord, if you had been here, my brother would not have died."

READING

117

I am generous and humble in heart. I pursue you and call you by name. There are times when difficulty comes that you hide your face from me. You stay with the crowd seeking to be comforted by them in ways only I am capable.

I know your sadness. I call you by name as you cry out.

Come to me.

I call for you because I know what you need and I want you to turn to me.

Come to me. Find me. Look for me as your source of comfort and care.

When you get up and turn to me be not afraid of your honest thoughts. I know that my ways are bigger than your understanding. Do not think you must come to me without doubt, anger, or grief. Bring your honest self to my feet. I know you blame me when difficulties come. I know you question my goodness. I know you doubt my character and love for you.

Come to me with these beliefs.

Come to me with clinch fists.

Come to me with raw emotion.

I will always meet you there. I will always welcome you. I will always be your comfort.

When your life feels pain or when you watch others know deep sadness, know I am looking for you, calling you by name and inviting you to come.

What do you hear?

LIVE

How will you respond?

A prompt for living

Be an extension of the comfort of Jesus to a person experiencing grief of any kind. Buy flowers, show up unexpected, leave a package, send a gift card for a meal, bake cookies, watch a movie with, sit quietly with, or simply speak to their grief, pain, or sadness. Extend comfort in the name of Jesus as you extend presence with your life and generosity.

LISTEN
John 11:33-36

³³ When Jesus saw her weeping, and the Jews who had come along with her also weeping, he was deeply moved in spirit and troubled. ³⁴ "Where have you laid him?" he asked. "Come and see, Lord," they replied. ³⁵ Jesus wept. ³⁶ Then the Jews said, "See how he loved him!

I love you. I love the exact way you were created. I carefully crafted your form. I pieced together each element of your personality. I skillfully designed each part.

My beloved you were made on purpose. You were made with intention. You were made skillfully and wonderfully. You can know that full well. Not one part of you was hidden from me. Before you lived a day, I knew you. I love you.

Your life displays my glory. Even those who do not call me by name or believe in my Son display our image. When you believe, your life becomes a bright light, telling my story and shining my fame.

My love is evident.

This is not stolen when you go through difficulty. In fact, my love is made more visible when you walk through struggle.

Hold to my love for you. Let it be your strength. Embrace my love when you experience life and death, for in my love you will know true life and your life will shine my glory.

Reading
118

What do
you hear?

LIVE

How will
you respond?

A prompt
for living

Write a card or email to a friend describing the great love Jesus has for them and the incredible intention he had when creating them.

LISTEN
John 11:37-39

37 But some of them said, "Could not he who opened the eyes of the blind man have kept this man from dying?" 38 Jesus, once more deeply moved, came to the tomb. It was a cave with a stone laid across the entrance. 39 "Take away the stone," he said. "But, Lord," said Martha, the sister of the dead man, "by this time there is a bad odor, for he has been there four days."

There is a way of man and there is my way. When you seek to understand me and what I ask of you with your own mind and understanding, you will continue to be puzzled. For my way is not yours. My thoughts and yours are so vastly different.

I know that you often struggle with the ideas of faith and responsibility. My ways can seem irresponsible to you. Sometimes I ask you to participate in things that will cause discomfort for you or others. You react to this as you worship comfort.

Trust me in this. When I ask something of you that goes against logic, comfort, or human nature, look to me and believe. I always have a larger view in mind.

I have a way that is beyond your capability to think or see.

My glory is revealed in impossibility. Your knowledge and skill are revealed through your own understanding and capability.

Seek first me, my kingdom and my way. Believe in me and step into each invitation to act with faith.

READING
119

What do you hear?

LIVE

How will you respond?

A prompt for living

Can you think of a time when you've felt prompted by Jesus to act in faith?

Share that story with a friend.

If you cannot think of a time where you've felt prompted by Jesus to act in any way, ask around. Is there anyone in your life who acts in faith? Sit down with them and ask how they learned to listen and respond to Him.

40 Then Jesus said, "Did I not tell you that if you believe, you will see the glory of God?"

41 So they took away the stone. Then Jesus looked up and said, "Father, I thank you that you have heard me. 42 I knew that you always hear me, but I said this for the benefit of the people standing here, that they may believe that you sent me." 43 When he had said this, Jesus called in a loud voice, "Lazarus, come out!" 44 The dead man came out, his hands and feet wrapped with strips of linen, and a cloth around his face. Jesus said to them, "Take off the grave clothes and let him go."

In me the long awaited life and healing is yours for I am the very source of life and good. When you believe in me, I bring life. I bring life to the very crevasses of darkness and death that continue to suffocate you. There are places within you where you've chosen to believe that which kills, steals, and destroys. Hold not longer to these things.

When I bring you new life do not continue to dress as one who walks in death. I've healed you. Take off the garments that covered your shame. Take off that which bound you. Take off that which hides and walk out into light, walk into life!

It is fear that keeps you from walking fully in your healing. It is disbelief that keeps you from living into the life I've given. I am the very source of life. It is not out of my hands to breathe new life into any dead thing. When you experience this, do not waste one moment of time by doubting my work or living in the familiar bondage of your burial clothes. Strip them off and jump into the covering of life. It is a beautiful gift.

What do you hear?

LIVE

How will you respond?

A prompt for living

Go through your closet and rid yourself of all the clothes you hold on to but do not use.

Take these clothes to your favorite thrift store. As you drop them off thank the Lord for giving you new garments of life in Him.

LISTEN
John 11:45-47

45 Therefore many of the Jews who had come to visit Mary, and had seen what Jesus did, believed in him. 46 But some of them went to the Pharisees and told them what Jesus had done. 47 Then the chief priests and the Pharisees called a meeting of the Sanhedrin.

Do you have eyes to see what I do? It is easy to go through life without noticing me. It's also easy to explain me away. Possibly you've witnessed a miracle and convinced yourself it was only a coincidence. Perhaps you've seen the work of my hand and instead of seeing me, you only saw nature or creativity. Maybe you experienced an awe inspiring sunset and instead of seeing me and being drawn to belief you only saw the color.

Every good gift is evidence of me.

Every happenstance of good, is really evidence of my divine intervention.

When there is no possible way out, and you find a way out, it is me.

When the provision comes, the healing takes place, and the rest is found, it is no mere work of humanity or the cosmos. NO! It is the work of the one who made humanity and crafted the cosmos.

Let all the good you see draw you to deeper belief in me.

I am here. I am at work. My love for you is incredibly detailed. Believe and receive every good and perfect gift as though it were gift wrapped from me to you.

READING
121

What do you hear?

LIVE

How will you respond?

A prompt for living

Call up five friends. Ask them to dinner. Around the table, ask them what good they've experienced in the past two weeks. Celebrate God's goodness in your lives as you break bread together!

⁴⁸ If we let him go on like this, everyone will believe in him, and then the Romans will come and take away both our temple and our nation." ⁴⁹ Then one of them, named Caiaphas, who was high priest that year, spoke up, "You know nothing at all! ⁵⁰ You do not realize that it is better for you that one man die for the people than that the whole nation perish." ⁵¹ He did not say this on his own, but as high priest that year he prophesied that Jesus would die for the Jewish nation, ⁵² and not only for that nation but also for the scattered children of God, to bring them together and make them one. ⁵³ So from that day on they plotted to take his life. ⁵⁴ Therefore Jesus no longer moved about publicly among the people of Judea. Instead he withdrew to a region near the wilderness, to a village called Ephraim, where he stayed with his disciples. ⁵⁵ When it was almost time for the Jewish Passover, many went up from the country to Jerusalem for their ceremonial cleansing before the Passover. ⁵⁶ They kept looking for Jesus, and as they stood in the temple courts they asked one another, "What do you think? Isn't he coming to the festival at all?" ⁵⁷ But the chief priests and the Pharisees had given orders that anyone who found out where Jesus was should report it so that they might arrest him.

There are those who speak my words and truth without their knowledge. My truth does not only come from those who know me. Listen for me in all things. I am at work and I will use whatever voice or circumstance necessary to tell my story.

When you get to know me and my word, you will recognize my words and truth when spoken. Therefore, let my word dwell in you richly. Let me be your source of teaching as opposed to person or particular church. Come to me. Become one with my word, and allow my Spirit to be your teacher.

People are conduits of my truth, they are not the source of truth. When a person or ideology becomes your truth, you are entrusting yourself to a false god.

Entrust yourself to me. Come to me. Listen to me in these things. You will recognize truth when it is spoken. Depend on me. Lean in to my truth. Surround yourself with words of life and you will begin to see me and hear me in the most unexpected places!

**What do
you hear?**

LIVE

**How will
you respond?**

**A prompt
for living**

Choose one attribute of God. Throughout your day, keep track of all the various ways you encounter that particular attribute. Invite a friend to do it with you. (Even if he or she doesn't know Jesus, they would be able to notice when good, beauty, truth, restoration, power, majesty or love is encountered) At the end of the day or week, share your lists with each other. Pray that Jesus will reveal himself through his character revealed.

JOHN 12 (Readings 123–139)

LISTEN
John 12:1-2

¹ Six days before the Passover, Jesus came to Bethany, where Lazarus lived, whom Jesus had raised from the dead. ² Here a dinner was given in Jesus' honor. Martha served, while Lazarus was among those reclining at the table with him.

I have done great things among you. I have risen the dead. I have healed the sick. I have met financial needs and I have been a constant presence in the most dark of places.

I am found in the miracle.

I have also done great things that often go unnoticed. I desire to sit with you; to meet with you as you gather together. I am with you. My very presence is a great gift and a beautiful miracle.

I come to you. I join you as you work, as you eat, as you laugh, as you play. I am with you on the river. I am with you behind the desk. I am with you at your table. I am with you in your home and I am with you in all your comings and goings. This is a great and beautiful miracle.

Do you see me?

Do you know that I am here?

Take this moment to sit with deep belief that I am here with you, even now as you read. I am here.

Breathe in and expect me.

I am not only found in the impossible moments of life, where you fall to your knees and look for me.

I am also there in your every day. I have given the miracle of my presence and I recline with you.

Look for me there. Look for me and I will be found. For I always reveal myself when you seek me with all of your heart!

What do you hear?

LIVE

How will you respond?

A prompt for living

Go to a place where there are forgotten people. It could be a neighbor, a particular street, a nursing home, an old friend. The options unfortunately are endless. Pray that Jesus will burden your heart for a particular place and people. Go to them and look for Jesus among them. Make a practice of seeing Jesus in the midst of the forgotten. As you do this, you will help others to know too, that Jesus sits with them.

LISTEN
John 12:3

³ Then Mary took about a pint of pure nard, an expensive perfume; she poured it on Jesus' feet and wiped his feet with her hair. And the house was filled with the fragrance of the perfume.

The fragrance of worship changes every space it touches. When my people worship me with their voices, the very walls take on the action of worship.

When you worship me with your service, those served in worship, are changed.

When you worship me with your love, the lives you touch are changed.

When you worship me with your thoughts, I take your thoughts captive and you change from the inside.

When you worship me in your world, I will be glorified and people will know my life altering presence.

Worship changes things, for worship places me in the center and fill the space with my love, grace, beauty, and restoration.

Worship lifts me up and I bring you with me. When you worship me, I inhabit your praise, and I make all things new in you and around you.

Grow to expect change, restoration, grace, love, healing, freedom, and glory when you worship me.

Grow to expect that your worship is more than a song, but it is a way of living in response to me. I am good and right and perfect and I will always respond to those who worship me, by changing them for the better.

Reading
124

What do you hear?

LIVE

How will you respond?

A prompt for living

Ask God what worship looks like for you today. Submit your day to His leading, His way and His care.

Act in response to your worship as God leads you.

LISTEN
John 12:4-8

4 But one of his disciples, Judas Iscariot, who was later to betray him, objected, 5 "Why wasn't this perfume sold and the money given to the poor? It was worth a year's wages." 6 He did not say this because he cared about the poor but because he was a thief; as keeper of the money bag, he used to help himself to what was put into it. 7 "Leave her alone," Jesus replied. "It was intended that she should save this perfume for the day of my burial. 8 You will always have the poor among you, but you will not always have me."

Oh dear one my heart aches for the world. Do you not see the need? Do you not realize that the world needs me more than any other thing.

I will always remember the story of this woman who poured out expensive perfume on my Son. Her gift was not wasted. The gift was a sacrifice of worship. She lavished me with this valuable gift and it was good. Her offering she declared that I worthy of the most precious of gifts and the most valuable of treasures.

Like Judas, there will be those who watch as you give to me and complain. Many may point fingers as though you've been selfish or foolish with your generosity. Still others may say that you have sinned against me, for your gift didn't come in the way they saw fit.

When you give to me, listen to me first. Know what I ask of you and give it generously.

Do not weigh the opinions of men—simply give. The world will be filled with your generosity and many will praise me as a result.

Trust in me. The needs of this world are met as people lavish me with their generosity.

What do you hear?

LIVE

How will you respond?

A prompt for living

Ask Jesus where he would like you to invest for His Kingdom with your belongings. Make a commitment to Jesus, to faithfully give all that He commands and bless others by loving Jesus with your generosity.

LISTEN
John 12:9

⁹ Meanwhile a large crowd of Jews found out that Jesus was there and came, not only because of him but also to see Lazarus, whom he had raised from the dead.

When I do marvelous things, there is no other response than amazement. When you drive through the mountains, walk along the sea, travel down rivers and watch the sun set in glorious splendor; your only response is amazement.

When you feel your heart beat, hold a tiny newborn, watch athletes run swift, and learn of the great intricacies of the human body, there is no other response than to be amazed.

When you walk through the most difficult of circumstances, when your heart is mended, when you were kept from trouble, when you barely escaped death's door, you can only stand in awe.

When you stand in the valley of the shadow of death, you know my presence, for I am your protection and your footing. When you walk through the raging waters and do not drown or you walk through the fire and do not burn, I am your protection. You can only be amazed.

When you've gone through the worst. When all is lost. When the darkness feels so overwhelmingly dark; my promise to you is that the darkness is not dark to me—in fact the darkness shines like the day. When you find breath and moments of peace as you walk this road; you can only see my hand and be amazed for I've not abandoned you.

Share the stories of my hand, and as you remember, you will be amazed just as all who hear.

READING

126

What do you hear?

LIVE

How will you respond?

A prompt for living

Think of a time when you were in awe of God.

Take a short moment to thank God for His work and then think of a friend who could use some encouragement. Take them out and share your story with them.

[10] So the chief priest made plans to kill Lazarus as well, [11] for on account of him many of the Jews were going over to Jesus and believe in him.

I am a threat to those who desire life to go only their way. I am a threat to those who worship their idea of god over the truth of who I am. This is not only true of a world who loves to serve false gods, but it is true of you as well.

There are times when you have no desire for me to come and transform you. Your desire is for life to be as you know it. You want life to be full of comfort, self advancement, ease, and success. You do not want a life of sacrifice, a life where even your greatest dreams are submitted to me, a life where I am Lord of all.

You hear stories of those who have submitted their lives in a costly way and make excuses why I will never ask that of you. You've taken me and have given me a new image when what I ask of you conflicts with self interest.

The truth is that I am good and only I am good. When you submit fully to me, you are giving yourself to a God who is perfect in all of His ways; a God who cares more about your good than your comfort; a God who longs for you to be transformed; a God who wants all of you, every last part.

Your belief is found in your submission to my loving care, my bountiful way, and my life altering truth. Let not any part of you worship a god of comfort, fame, security, safety or success. In these things you will not find life, you will only find paths that lead you away from me. Believe in me and submit in all of your ways; it is only here that you will find life for today and every tomorrow to come.

What do you hear?

LIVE

How will you respond?

A prompt for living

Think of something within your cultural context that is an idol or place of worship to a lesser god: education, money, success, sports, physical health, and the like. Go to a place of worship: a gym, a bank, the business district, a sports field, or a school and walk around the block, building, or neighborhood praying that God will bring himself to those who worship false gods. Pray that God would give you a heart for those who live a lesser god. Pray that you will constantly point others to Jesus as the one true God!

> *¹² The next day the great crowd that had come for the festival heard that Jesus was on his way to Jerusalem. ¹³ They took palm branches and went out to meet him; shouting, "Hosanna!" Blessed is he who comes in the name of the Lord! Blessed is the king of Israel!" ¹⁴ Jesus found a young donkey and sat on it, as it is written: ¹⁵ "Do not be afraid, Daughter Zion; see, your king is coming seated on a donkey's colt."*

To you I am an upside down God. I do things so contrary to human logic. I reveal myself not as you think I should, but as I know to be best. I am subtle when you think loud works best and I am grand when only small is requested.

It is not yours to know why, but it is yours to believe in me. Oh my love, look for me and worship me. The echo of your worship will dance through the cosmos joining the symphony of creation whose job is to continually lift up my name.

Hosanna! Hosanna! A word created only for me. *Glory* and *Blessing* are words only accurately used when attached to my name.

I am matchless in every way. I am full of good. I am abounding in grace and I love to hear my children sing. I dance along with your words.

Yes, my love, I at times come on stallions and other times I come on donkeys. It is not the conduit that brings me which is to be searched out, no it is me. So seek me. Believe I am to be found. Watch, look, and listen and I who am God will awaken you to me.

What do you hear?

LIVE

How will you respond?

A prompt for living

Grab a friend and for one week, together, keep track of every way you encountered the character of God. Share your lists at the end of the week over a cup of coffee and celebrate God's daily revelation and his matchless character!

LISTEN
John 12:16

16 At first his disciples did not understand all this. Only after Jesus was glorified did they realize that these things had been written about him and that these things had been done to him.

Beloved, I know that it often takes months, and many times years to understand the deep truths of my work in the world, my work in your life. I am always at work. I am continually developing and shaping you. It is mine to lead you on the journey of belief.

For some, the road is filled with obstacles. For others, their road seems short. My work is beyond human understanding and timing. I am at work constantly. Not a second goes by that I am not about the work of revelation. Oh my beloved, trust that I am walking with those you love. Trust that I am at work in you. Trust that I am aware of your need for security. I know your needs because I created you with them.

I know your desires, for I created you intentionally with every want, hope, and deep longing.

I know your cravings that are never satisfied in this world, because I made you to crave things only I can fill. Oh my love, let your cravings lead you to me. Pray that your friend's cravings will lead them to me as well.

I know it will take time. The arch of my love is much longer than your timeline.

Trust that I am at work. Participate in my kingdom by walking with others on their journey to belief. Do not worry. I do not judge on timing. Continue your journey of faith. Continue seeking me. Continue to place yourself and your desires under my watchful care and know that I am a loving patient God who celebrates every step.

READING
129

**What do
you hear?**

LIVE

**How will
you respond?**

**A prompt
for living**

Do you have a friend you've prayed for years that they'd come to know Jesus or that they'd turn to follow him again? Write that person a card today, simply telling them that you love them and that you are praying for them. Let your words be few, the love of Jesus great and the truth be palpable.

LISTEN
John 12:17-19

17 Now the crowd that was with him when he called Lazarus from the tomb and raised him from the dead continued to spread the word. 18 Many people, because they had heard that he had performed this sign, went out to meet him. 19 So the Pharisees said to one another, "see, this is getting us nowhere. Look how the whole world has gone after him!"

My kingdom is greater than any kingdom of this world. You may fret about what is to come in your own country. You may worry about my way being shoved out for the way of man. Fear not! My Spirit is in you and my Spirit is greater than anything this world can throw at you.

Yes, there are many who shun my way. There are many who have no desire to follow my way and even those who fight to keep my way from being lawful. Even these will not be able to stop my kingdom.

My kingdom is within you. My kingdom has come into this world and is at work. You participate in my kingdom when you follow my Son and his way. No leader, corporation, rebel group, enemy, man, or woman can steal my kingdom from within you, nor can they keep me from revealing myself to a watching world.

When the world wants to snuff me out, I burn brighter!

The stories of my work in the world will always lead some to me and others to fear, for they've put their hope in themselves and princes and kings, not in me or my Son.

When the world seems to be against me, trust me, look for me, tell my story and be my witness. You are the greatest light pointing others to me. Shine brightly! even when the world seems to love darkness.

Reading

130

What do you hear?

LIVE

How will you respond?

A prompt for living

Pray for those who lead in your city, state, and country. Find out the names of those who are in political positions around you and pray that God will reveal himself to them. Pray that God will heal them, grow them in wisdom and pray that you will grow in love for them as people who bear the image of their Creator. If you feel compelled, write an email or a card to thank them for their service and let them know that you pray for them.

LISTEN
John 12:20-22

²⁰ Now there were some Greeks among those who went up to worship at the festival. ²¹ They came to Philip, who was from Bethsaida in Galilee, with a request. "Sir," they said, we would like to see Jesus." ²² Philip went to tell Andrew; Andrew and Philip in turn told Jesus.

My love abounds in all countries, languages, and economic standings. My love is beyond present belief. My love is beyond lifestyle. My love is beyond public opinion. My love is vast and high and deep and wide. My love is for all. My love is great.

Be generous with stories of my love. Be generous with your love of others. Love so deeply that the hurt and rejection so many feel is healed as my loved flows through you.

Where there is rejection, love.

Where there is bigotry, love.

Where there is hopelessness, love.

Where there is hate, love.

Where there is discord, love.

Where there is depression, love.

Where there is racial tension, love.

Where there is animosity, love.

Where there are acts of violence, love.

Where there is hunger, love.

Where there is fear, love.

Where there is slavery, love

Where there is thirst, love.

Where there is drunkenness, love.

Where there is illness, love.

Where there are people, any people, be complete in your love for them.

For as you root yourself in my great and all encompassing love for you, I will love the world through you.

READING
131

What do you hear?

LIVE

How will you respond?

A prompt for living

Host an Agape dinner, a lavish, extraordinary, undeserved banquet for those in your life who do not deserve the generosity. Ask Jesus to love these people through you!

LISTEN
John 12:20-22

23 Jesus replied, "The hour has come for the Son of Man to be glorified. 24 Very truly I tell you, unless a kernel of wheat falls to the ground and dies, it remains only a single seed. But if it dies, it produces many seeds. 25 Anyone who loves their life will lose it, while anyone who hates their life in this world will keep it for eternal life. 26 Whoever serves me must follow me; and where I am, my servant also will be. My Father will honor the one who serves me.

Yes it is true my beloved, everything must die for it to know life. I know this is a hard teaching. I know that you cling to your life and your dreams. I know that you long for things and as a result you worship outcomes more than me. I know you want your life to be a certain way and you strive and strive to make this life happen. Oh my child I have so much more for you! Give all of those ideas up, lay them down, be willing to let them die, so that I can come in and breathe my life into you, into your dreams. It is by dying to your own life that I am invited in and I bring new life. I bring life that is hard to fathom, for it is beyond your wildest dreams.

Oh beloved, trust you life to me. Take your hands off the wheel, let go of the life you've created for yourself, let go of the life you want for yourself and come to me. Lay it down, let it die, grieve its loss, and look to me. I have been by your side every step of the way and I will continue to be. I will take your life and dreams and future and I will raise them up. I will give them new life. I will give life that can only be experienced as you follow me. It is only in dying to self that you are able to truly experience life. Yes, this again is an invitation to deep belief, for it is your greatest work. Will you die so that you can live?

Come, take hold of me and live.

What do you hear?

LIVE

How will you respond?

A prompt for living

Volunteer at a community garden. As you tend to the ground and plants in whatever stage they may be, remember that each seed planted dies before the crop is fruitful!

LISTEN
John 12:27-30

27 Now my soul is troubled, and what shall I say? Father, save me from this hour? No, it was for this very reason I came to this hour. 28 Father, glorify your name! Then a voice came from heaven. "I have glorified it, and will glorify it again." 29 The crowd that was there and heard it said it had thundered; others said an angel had spoken to him. 30 Jesus said, "This voice was for your benefit, not mine.

I want everyone everywhere to know my glory; because, I want everyone everywhere to know life, to have life. At times my glory is found in suffering. My very own son knew the hour of suffering. He knew that I must be glorified so that all people would know life and his suffering was a part of my glory.

I am constantly on display. I do not hide myself from those who do not believe. People see and hear with their own eyes and ears. Some witness a miracle and do not want to believe. Some misunderstand. Some hold so tightly to being right, that they miss me all together. And, some will see and believe. I will not stop revealing myself. I will stop putting my glory on display.

At times you may walk a very difficult path, when you do, ask me where I am. My promise is that I will be with you. I know at times it seems as though I do not hear or even answer your prayers. I know this often strains your faith. How can you believe in a god who doesn't rescue right away? I am not immune to your questions. But my view is much longer than yours. I know the result of the difficulty in your life and in the lives of those you love. Do not fight it, lean in to difficult circumstances and look for me. Ask how I may want to use these circumstances in your life or in the lives of those around you to bring glory to my name. Learn into me. I will be right there with you.

I know that even now you do not understand these things. The invitation once again is to trust. Trust that I AM, who is God, is good and right and perfect, and I will always do what is good and right and perfect. I will always display my glory in a way that is good and right and perfect. Trust in me and your life will display my glory even in your deepest sufferings.

**What do
you hear?**

LIVE

**How will
you respond?**

**A prompt
for living**

Is there a walkway that is stunningly beautiful near you? An art museum that has masterpieces on display? Invite a friend who is going through a difficult time to go experience this place with you. Ask Jesus to speak to your friend, and watch as he reveals himself. Leave your friend with the hope that He who creates good is with them as they walk this difficult road.

LISTEN
John 12:31-33

31 Now is the time for judgment on this world; now the prince of this world will be driven out. 32 And I, when I am lifted up from the earth, will draw all people to myself." 33 He said this to show the kind of death he was going to die.

I want you to know that it is my deepest desire to draw all people to myself and to drive out the evil one from every corner of this earth. I long for people to come to me, for I know it is in me that life is found. I watch as the prince of this world seeks to devour those I love. I see him lie to children and plant seeds of self-contempt, loneliness, hatred, and inadequacy. I see him affirm lies in those I love as they grow. I see people search for meaning and want to know love. I watch them turn to false sources to meet these deepest needs. I watch hearts break. I hear desperate cries. I feel the pain of those I love. The prince of this world loves to kill, steal, and destroy; it is his greatest pleasure to watch life come to ruin.

Too often you have believed his lies. You have held onto self-contempt as though it were your own truth. You look for ways to affirm the fact that your life has little value and you seek to find value and love in sources other than me. You go to others, things, activities, and even your own self to satisfy your deepest longings for identity and value.

I tell you the truth. I am the way. I am truth. I am life. It is only in me that the prince of this world is destroyed and it is only in me that you will know value and identity. You cannot find life apart from me. You cannot find hope apart from me. You cannot work hard enough, do enough good, be liked by enough people, make enough money, or own enough stuff to find value. Come to me as you are weary of these lies. Come to me as you need the restoration I alone can bring. Come to me as your source. Come to me, I will give you rest.

Reading
134

What do you hear?

LIVE

How will you respond?

A prompt for living

Write a letter to your pastor reminding him or her of their value source. Speak words of life outside of performance. Speak words of hope based on the character of Jesus. Speak words of love based on the life of Savior Jesus. Speak words of truth based on the very truth of Jesus. Pray that God will give you exact words to encourage him or her today.

LISTEN
John 12:34-36

34 The crowd spoke up, "We have heard from the Law that the Messiah will remain forever, so how can you say, 'The Son of Man must be lifted up?' Who is this 'Son of Man'?" 35 Then Jesus told them, "You are going to have the light just a little while longer. Walk while you have the light, before darkness overtakes you. Whoever walks in the dark does not know where they are going. 36 Believe in the light while you have the light, so that you may become children of the light." When he had finished speaking, Jesus left and hid himself from them.

Your questions are important to me. I see behind them to the fear and misguided beliefs that often rule within you. You often question, to blame me, not to understand me. I am gentle and humble in heart and I see your fear. I feel your subtle blame. I know that you have unmet expectations. I am not afraid of these things. I do not judge you for them. I simply desire to draw you out of these places of fear and blame and deception.

When you ask questions of me, I will answer you. My answers will speak to the matters of your heart, which are often not the same as the question asked. Listen carefully when I speak. Listen carefully as I teach. Look and listen for me when I respond to you. It will always be my desire to draw you out of the darkness of fear, blame and deception and invite you to walk with me in truth, to walk with me in light. I want you to walk in light.

I am light. In me there is absolutely no darkness. I am light. In me there is no despair. I am light. In me there is no death. I am light. In me there is no fear. I am light. In me there is no place for blame. I am light. In me there is no deception.

I am light. Walk with me, walk in the light.

What do you hear?

LIVE

How will you respond?

A prompt for living

Get a group of friends together and collect lanterns and flashlights and book lights. Go to a place nearby where there are those who live in actual darkness and give them light. As you hand out the lanterns, flashlights, and book lights be ready to answer the question "why are you doing this?"

LISTEN
John 12:37-41

37 Even after Jesus had performed so many signs in their presence, they still would not believe in him. 38 This was to fulfill the word of Isaiah the prophet: "Lord, who has believed our message and to whom has the arm of the Lord been revealed?" 39 For this reason they could not believe, because, as Isaiah says elsewhere: 40 "He has blinded their eyes and hardened their hearts, so they can neither see with their eyes, nor understand with their hearts, nor turn—and I would heal them." 41 Isaiah said this because he saw Jesus' glory and spoke about him.

Grace. Grace is needed to see, to believe, to understand, to receive. Grace is undeserved and it is freely given. There are those who do not want the grace I have to give. They want to earn understanding. They want to earn salvation. They've come to believe that they are the source of their own destiny.

Grace is undeserved. Grace is given, but is not forced. Some will choose to accept the grace that is offered and others will walk their own way.

Grace was offered in the very beginning. I gave grace in the garden. I gave life in the garden. I created a tree of life where man could eat freely and taste life itself.

But, the allure of knowledge, the allure of the ability to judge, the allure of becoming like me was too great and Adam and Eve chose judgment over grace.

You too have the same opportunity. You can choose grace or you can choose judgment. Your choice will determine how you view things. You may see signs and wonders and believe in me or you may see signs and wonders and make judgments to rationalize their existence. You were not created with the ability to judge and it is judgment itself that keeps you from loving and from receiving love. Choose grace over judgment. Choose life over darkness. Choose belief over unbelief and you will know the grace given in the tree of life.

What do you hear?

LIVE

How will you respond?

A prompt for living

Give something today that is underserved and without expectation.

LISTEN
John 12:42–43

42 Yet at the same time many even among the leaders believed in him. But because of the Pharisees they would not openly acknowledge their faith for fear they would be put out of the synagogue; 43 for they loved human praise more than praise from God.

Your fear is often misplaced. You say you believe in me. You say you believe in my Son and yet your choices often show that your fear is greater than your belief.

You fear the ridicule of man more than you believe that I have given you value as my child.

You fear harm to those you love, so you become angry at even the slightest possible harm, rather than believe that I protector and sovereign.

You fear running out of resources, so you store up treasures on earth, because you do not believe that I am provider.

You fear discomfort, so you've crafted a world where people respond to you as you want them to, where your surroundings are filled with pleasurable things, where you will never be without, because you do not believe that I am the God of comfort and the God of good who desires you to know His goodness more than human comfort.

You fear failure, so you do not risk, because you do not believe that you will be acceptable if you fall.

You fear success, so you hide your gift, because you do not believe that your gift is worth giving and that I will not be with you in your successes.

You fear things won't turn out in your situation, so you work hard, hide feelings, and grow weary trying, because you do not believe that I am for you and for good in your situation.

You fear intimacy, so you become inauthentic, because you do not believe that my love for you is enough and that even your deepest secrets are not too much for me.

Your reactions, responses, choices, and behaviors are indications of fear and belief. May your belief increase and may that which you fear be swallowed up by me, for I alone am good and right and perfect. Place your hope in me. Place your belief in me. And do not be afraid.

What do you hear?

LIVE

How will you respond?

A prompt for living

Is there good that you know you are to do and have not because you've been afraid for various reasons? Today, place your belief in Jesus and step out, doing the good you've avoided out of fear.

READING
137

LISTEN
John 12:44-46

44 Then Jesus cried out, "Whoever believes in me does not believe in me only, but in the one who sent me. 45 The one who looks at me is seeing the one who sent me. 46 I have come into the world as a light, so that no one who believes in me should stay in darkness.

My son is the exact representation of me. When you look on him, you see him. When you hear his story, you know my story. When you learn of his great love for you, you know my great love for you. My love for you is beyond understanding, for I gave you the gift of my Son. He is the light. When you believe in him you embrace the light and you step out of darkness.

Darkness is found everywhere in this world. Light is found only in my Son, because he is the light. I am the light.

When you know darkness, look to my Son.

When you know sadness, look to my Son.

When your life has been uprooted, look to my Son.

When you have no answers, look to my Son.

When you do not have hope, look to my Son.

When you are lost, look to my Son.

When you are lonely, look to my Son.

Let his light surround you and bring hope, joy, peace, goodness, kindness, gentleness, and freedom. Let my light shine brightly around you. Let my light shine in your home. Let my light lift you out of the pit. Cling to the darkness no more, cling to me! Embrace my light. Embrace my Son. Believe in him. Yes, again I say believe. It is the cry of my every word to you! Believe in my Son! Believe and you will walk in light.

Reading
138

What do you hear?

LIVE

How will you respond?

A prompt for living

Host a dinner party with only candles for light. Place on the table small cards with various attributes of Jesus. Ask people to share to pick one attribute that has been light in their life this past month.

⁴⁷ If anyone hears my words but does not keep them, I do not judge that person. For I did not come to judge the world, but to save the world. ⁴⁸ There is a judge for the one who rejects me and does not accept my words; the very words I have spoken will condemn them at the last day. ⁴⁹ For I did not speak on my own, but the Father who sent me commanded me to say all that I have spoken. ⁵⁰ I know that his command leads to eternal life. So whatever I say is just what the Father has told me to say.

I am the Creator of life. I know how life works. I know what will bring life and I know what will destroy life. I am a good God. I am a gracious God. I am a perfect God. I am all knowing, all loving, all compassionate, and I am the great I AM.

It is for your sake that I sent my Son to share with you about life. It is for your good that I have given my one and only son. It is for your life both now and for eternity that my Son spoke my words of truth and life. Follow after him. He is the way. He is the truth and He is the life.

I say this, because I created life. Life only existed in me before I gave breath to all living things. My way is not a way of legalistic restriction. NO! My way is not a way of reckless abandon. NO! My way is free. My way is complete. My way takes every person into consideration and my way always gives life. My way never robs life.

If you follow a false way, you will only know rules, worry, and selfish ambition. But my way, as seen in my Son, always gives dignity, compassion, grace, mercy, love, and always, ALWAYS my way gives life.

Reading

139

What do you hear?

LIVE

How will you respond?

A prompt for living

Do you have a friend who is an expert at something? Ask if you can learn from them. Or perhaps you and a friend can go on a tour, take a class, or learn from someone who is an expert. As you learn, be reminded of the fact that Jesus created life and is the expert on life. Talk this fact over with your friend. How does it affect your understanding of the way of Jesus if you know he is the expert at living fully and abundantly?

JOHN 13   (Readings 140–149)

¹ It was just before the Passover Festival. Jesus knew that the hour had come for him to leave this world and to go to the Father. Having loved his own who were in the world, he loved them to the end.

My love is complete. I do not give up on loving you. I do not tire of loving you. I do not throw in the towel or throw my hands up in surrender. My love for you is until the very end.

Trust this! What good news. I am your greatest and most complete lover. I know you. I formed you. I've walked with you. I have sat with you. I have cried with you and I have cried for you. I have been with you on the wings of the dawn and I have been with you on the far side of the sea. I have been with you to the greatest heights and your greatest depths. I have not abandoned you one time and my love for you has never run dry.

I am the lover of your soul.

I will love you for all of eternity.

Rest in my love. Rejoice in it. Soak in it. Let the thought of me, the God of the Universe, loving you just as you are right at this moment come over you. As you sit in this glorious thought bring to me all of the places where you have felt my love could not reach.

Bring to my your brokenness. Bring to me your pride. Bring to me your fear. Bring to me your deceit. Bring to me your wants. Bring to me your anger. Bring to me your disappointments. Bring to me all of you and let my love, my complete love wash over every part. As my love touches you in your depths, ask me to transform you to live out of my love. Celebrate. Rejoice. Be glad. For I, the God of the Universe love you completely.

READING
140

What do you hear?

LIVE

How will you respond?

A prompt for living

Sometimes it is just nice to hear the words I love you. Today use those three words generously. Speak of Jesus' love over all those with whom you come in contact. Pray the love of Jesus over every person you see.

LISTEN
John 13:2-5

2 The evening meal was in progress, and the devil had already prompted Judas, the son of Simon Iscariot, to betray Jesus. 3 Jesus knew that the Father had put all things under his power and that he had come from God and was returning to God; 4 so he got up from the meal, took off his outer clothing, and wrapped a towel around his waist. 5 After that, he poured water into a basin and began to wash his disciples' feet, drying them with the towel that was wrapped around him.

The meal was under way. I had given my Son everything. All things had been placed under his power. He knows my way is generous, even to those who I know will never believe and to those who spit at the very sound of my name. He knows that sacrifice is a beautiful expression of love.

Imagine you were at the table as the scene unfolds. He takes his outer robe off and gets on his hands and knees and washes the dirt, filth and sewage from the long day's walk off the feet of those who for years had followed him. He was their teacher. He was their leader and yet He touched the filth and washed each one and made them clean.

My son, lives in me, and my power was shown that day as he encountered filth and made it clean. It is in my Son that all will be made clean. It is by his power, power which I've placed all things under, that all men and women everywhere are able to be washed and made clean.

You, my child, often believe that there are some parts of you that cannot be cleansed by my gracious, generous love. My son is the exact representation of me and my way and he came to every man at the table knelt down and washed away their filth. This is the same generous love that I give you every day. Believe that it is my desire that you be clean, that you be made whole. Believe that I have created a way for you that is not found in your performance, but found in the work of my Son, my beloved son. Trust that he will do the work and believe that you too are the recipient of lavish generosity.

What do you hear?

LIVE

How will you respond?

A prompt for living

What is a job or chore that is hated by your family, co-workers, or roommate? Do this chore as an expression of extravagant love, expecting nothing in return, not even a thank you. Pray for those you are serving as you accomplish this task. Pray that they will know and accept the lavish, generous, love of Jesus and be transformed by it!

LISTEN
John 13:6-9

⁶ He came to Simon Peter, who said to him, "Lord, are you going to wash my feet?" ⁷ Jesus replied, "You do not realize now what I am doing, but later you will understand." ⁸ "No," said Peter, "you shall never wash my feet." Jesus answered, "Unless I wash you, you have no part with me." ⁹ "Then, Lord," Simon Peter replied, "not just my feet but my hands and my head as well!"

My ways are not your ways. My thoughts are not your thoughts. You know a way that seems right. I know what is right. I know what is good. I only do that which is perfect. You question this at times. You do not understand why things are playing out as they are and you question my sovereignty. Trust is needed when you do not understand.

Everything I do has purpose. Everything I do has great intension. Everything I do is for your good. I know you do not understand this. I know that you think there are things you must earn or things you accomplish for me. This is not grace, this is not of me. Broken people have been your teachers and at times they have taught out of their own understanding and not out of the truth of my way or my character. I know this has hurt you. I know this has skewed the way you think of me and my way. Let go of these teachings and come again to me. Do not blame those who taught you out of their own misunderstanding. Do not allow anger and bitterness to rise up within you. Instead, come to me.

Come to me with your brokeness, misunderstandings, strivings, work, and place yourself under my complete care. Let go of the teachings that say you must become clean to come to me. Let go of the teachings that you are undeserving of lavish love, and believe that I am holding out on you. Let go of the teachings that your behavior is crucial to receive from my generous and unconditional love. Let go of these and let my Spirit be your teacher. I will never lead you astray. When human ways have hurt you, come to me, take hold of me, and live out of me.

My beloved, trust me in this. Trust me when you do not understand. Trust me. I will complete my work in you.

What do you hear?

LIVE

How will you respond?

A prompt for living

Today, ask Holy Spirit to show you where you have bitterness towards the church, mentors, or teachers that taught you out of their brokenness and misguided belief.
Make a list and make a conscious choice to forgive each person or institution. Say it aloud. I forgive _____ for _____ and in the power of Jesus I let go of any bitterness that has taken root in me and I choose to love instead.

READING
142

LISTEN
John 13:10-11

¹⁰ Jesus answered, "those who have had a bath need only to wash their feet; their whole body is clean. And you are clean, though not every one of you." ¹¹ For he knew who was going to betray him, and that was why he said not every one was clean.

I know that you are clean. I know that you have rooted yourself in me. I know that you find your hope in me. I know that you are with me and believe in me. I know that you believe in my Son. I know that you believe I am at work. I know that you want your life to reflect my glory and I know that you desire to participate in my kingdom.

I know too that at times your belief wavers. I know too that there are moments when you trust more in yourself and your own abilities than me. I know that you stumble and fall. I know this will always be while you are on this earth.

My saving work is once and for all. I have completed this work in you. You do not need to worry. You do not need to come for healing over and over again as if my work were incomplete or temperamental.

There are times where you lose sight of me, come to me in those times and ask to be reminded of my work in you.

Come to me when you've forgotten hope and ask me to wash away your despair.

Come back to me when you've walked away and allow my grace to wash over your wandering.

Come to me when you have ignored your healing and I will remind you that you are well. There is no shame to be found in relationship with me. There is only grace, love, and restoration. I have made you clean, and well and free—walk in it.

What do you hear?

LIVE

How will you respond?

A prompt for living

Do you know one who follows Jesus yet continues to live in shame? Ask Jesus to give you scriptures and words for them. Write a card to them expressing the truth Jesus sees and give it to them! Pray that God free them from the shame that they walk in and believe for them that God will free them of shames bondage.

12 When he had finished washing their feet, he put on his clothes and returned to his place. "Do you understand what I have done for you?" He asked them. 13 "You call me 'Teacher' and 'Lord,' and rightly so, for that is what I am. 14 Now that I, your Lord and Teacher have washed your feet you also should wash one another's feet. 15 I have set you an example that you should do as I have done for you. 16 Very truly I tell you, no servant is greater than his master, nor is a messenger greater than the one who sent him. 17 Now that you know these things, you will be blessed if you do them.

Because I served you first, you are able to serve. Because I loved you first, you are able to love. Because I was generous with you first, you are able to be generous. I do not ask anything of you that I do not myself do first.

I have given my very son for you as your example, as your way, as the truth to which you hold, and as your very source of life. This is my greatest gift of love. My son is the perfect expression of my love for you.

He gave his life out of love for you.
He served out of love for you.
He spoke out of love for you.

His motivation at all times was love for me and love for you.

When he gave he did so out of these two loves.

He was obedient to me out of love for me and he served you out of love for you.

You too are invited to live in a similar way.

Serve because you believe I am good and you believe my commands are for your good. Serve out of obedience drenched in love for me and selfless actions of kindness for others smothered in love for people. As you do, you will know my blessing.

READING
144

**What do
you hear?**

LIVE

**How will
you respond?**

**A prompt
for living**

Today perform a random act of kindness. Ask the Jesus give you eyes to see need and that you would see where someone needs encouragement, hope, or a simple random provision. Without anyone knowing, do something kind for another out of love for Jesus and the person you choose to serve.

LISTEN
John 13:18–21

18 I am referring to all of you; I know those I have chosen. But this is to fulfill this passage of Scripture: 'He who shared my bread has turned against me.' 19 I am telling you now before it happens, so that when it does happen you will believe that I am who I am. 20 Very truly I tell you, whoever accepts anyone I send accepts me; and whoever accepts me accepts the one who sent me.' 21 After he had said this, Jesus was troubled in spirit and testified, "Very truly I tell you, one of you is going to betray me.

READING

145

It is hard to know what to say when you come against those who turn against me. Your heart aches as the world and many who say they follow me turn against me to serve other gods. Some, even now, say they follow me, but they serve a god made in their own image.

I know this angers you. I know you grow so disheartened as you see those who say they follow, actually lead people in another way. Do not grow bitter towards me when those who say they represent me, turn. Do not hold ongoing anger towards those who betray me in front of others.

Bitterness towards me and others will get you nowhere as it will only push me away.

Oh dear one, can't you see? I am good, in me there resides no evil. In me there is love and tenderness and compassion. When you grow bitter towards me, because of man you only realize that at one time you served the wrong master. Men are not perfect. Men will fail. Women will betray and turn others against me. Your bitterness is an indication of where you placed your hope and where your expectations were not met.

Place your hope in me. Place your hope in my character. I will never fail you. Men and women and institutions will fail you. Your friends will fail you. You will feel betrayed. You will see others betray me. Do not lose heart! I have not, nor will I fail you. Run to me, come back to me, ask me to forgive your misplaced blame and bitterness and return to your first love.

What do you hear?

LIVE

How will you respond?

A prompt for living

Is there a person in your life who let you down or betrayed you in some way? Come to Jesus with that person, group, or institution and ask me to help you forgive them. If you are able, seek reconciliation with them.

²² His disciples stared at one another, at a loss to know which of them he meant. ²³ One of them, the disciple whom Jesus loved, was reclining next to him. ²⁴ Simon Peter motioned to this disciple and said, "Ask him which one he means." ²⁵ Leaning back against Jesus, he asked him, "Lord, who is it?" ²⁶ Jesus answered, "It is the one to whom I will give this piece of bread when I have dipped it in the dish." Then, dipping the piece of bread, he gave it to Judas, the son of Simon Iscariot. ²⁷ As soon as Judas took the bread, Satan entered into him. So Jesus told him, "what you are about to do, do quickly," ²⁸ But no one at the meal understood why Jesus said this to him. ²⁹ Since Judas had charge of the money some thought Jesus was telling him to buy what was needed for the festival, or to give something to the poor. ³⁰ As soon as Judas had taken the bread, he went out. And it was night.

You have an enemy. He desires to devour you, to destroy you. He takes great pleasure in watching you suffer. He only knows deception, for it is his language. He carefully schemes and works to lead you away from me and away from life. Be on your guard!

As you walk with me I will place my word in your heart. I will place my truth on your tongue. I will give you eyes to see and I will give you ears with which you'll hear. I have great love for you. I fiercely protect my children when they cry out for help.

Walk with me. I am the greatest defense against your enemies. I am your help in times of trouble. I am your truth. I am your way out. I am your life-line. Come to me.

When the enemy rises against you, come to me.

When he lies to you, let my word fight against his words.

When he is violent and when he attacks you with fear, do not be afraid. I am the Lord your God. I am Holy. I am just. I will protect you.

My beloved, take refuge in me, learn from me, know my voice, seek my heart and walk closely with me; these are your greatest defense against the enemy of your soul.

Be at peace. I am Lord.

What do you hear?

LIVE

How will you respond?

A prompt for living

Take a moment to speak words of truth and life over someone you know who struggles to believe good about herself. Speak these words in whatever way you believe will be the greatest encouragement.

READING
146

LISTEN
John 13:31-33

31 When he was gone, Jesus said, "Now the Son of Man is glorified and God is glorified in him. 32 If God is glorified in him, God will glorify the Son in himself, and will glorify him at once.

33 My children, I will be with you only a little longer. You will look for me and just as I told the Jews, so I will tell you now: Where I am going, you cannot come.

Glory is something you do not fully understand. Glory is from me and it is given to those who reveal me in this world. My son was glorified in me. You too are glorified in me. When you walk the way of obedience it is not you that is given honor, no it is me. I am given glory when you obediently follow me. I am given glory when you obediently risk.

I desire for you to know the glory that can only be found in me, because I know the taste of pure good and want you to share in it.

Walking with me is a journey of trust. As your belief increases, your trust in me increases and your life responds with obedience. My child, let my Spirit lead you. Listen for his still, small voice. Allow the promptings of my Spirit lead you to my glory, sharing in my pure good for you.

READING

147

What do you hear?

LIVE

How will you respond?

A prompt for living

Is there good you are to do in your life but have not done it for various reasons?
Is there a person who keeps popping into your mind? A letter to write? An act of service?
A relationship to reconcile? Do not hold off any longer! Do it!

³⁴ A new command I give you: Love one another. As I have loved you, so you must love one another. ³⁵ By this everyone will know that you are my disciples, if you love one another."

My Beloved, Love is my name. Love is at the core of my nature. Love is the most perfect expression of me in the world. Love is powerful. Love is pure. Love is generous. Love does not seek attention. Love is humble. Love does not hide. Love does not force. Love is full of grace. Love is full of truth. Love protects. Love always trusts. Love always has hope. Love is constant. Love is selfless. Love is strong. Love is gentle. Love is for now. Love leads to life. Love is free. Love is deep and high and wide and long. Love is absent of evil. Love is full of compassion. Love expresses itself in joy. Love likes. Love thinks of others before oneself. Love gives without needing anything in return. Love forgives. Love heals. Love is foolish to the world. Love is my wisdom embodied. Love smiles. Love cries. Love strengthens. Love walks with. Love is present. Love is kind. Love is thoughtful. Love does not envy. Love brings peace. Love casts out fear.

This is what obedience looks like: Love one another as my Son loves you, as I love you through him. Love deeply and generously. This kind of love is impossible without me.

Find yourself in me, rooted in my love for you and this love will grow in you and will flow from you.

READING
148

**What do
you hear?**

LIVE

**How will
you respond?**

**A prompt
for living**

Spend some good time with Jesus around this question. If there is any action that needs to take place as a result do what is prompted with in you.

Where is there a lack of love in your life: towards self? Friends? Your leaders? Family? Strangers? People in the media?

Confess your lack of love and ask God to grow in you a love that can only come from him. Ask God to give you compassion and grace for all people, everywhere.

LISTEN
John 13:36-38

³⁶ Simon Peter asked him, "Lord, where are you going? Jesus replied, "Where I am going you cannot follow now, but you will follow later." ³⁷ Peter asked, "Lord, why can't I follow you now? I will lay down my life for you." ³⁸ Then Jesus answered, "Will you really lay down your life for me? Very truly I tell you, before the rooster crows, you will disown me three times!"

Your grand gestures and declarations of impassioned commitment are a part of our relationship. But the depth of our relationship is a discovery often made not on the mountain, where your breath is taken away, but in the valley. In the very depths of life's most difficult moments you experience my love and presence in ways that give you your very breath.

As you walk with me, you will walk through dark seasons where you cannot seem to find me. You will also walk through times where you feel me as though I am as close as your own skin. At times you will know my voice and at other times the voice of the enemy will be louder than mine. Walk with me in all seasons and at all times. My desire is that you seek me and turn to me, even when it will cost you something on this earth.

Oh my beloved, do not be swayed by the world and the opinions of man, but seek me first. Walk with me through the valley. Soar with me on the heights. My love for you is great and vast beyond understanding. Trust, walk, and remain. I will be your very breath and I will be that which takes your breath away.

Reading
149

What do you hear?

LIVE

How will you respond?

A prompt for living

Invite a friend to go for a walk or a hike with you. As you walk ask where he feels he is in his own walk. Encourage him in some way to know that wherever in life's walk he find himself that God desires to walk with him.

John 14 (Readings 150–160)

LISTEN
John 14:1–3

"Do not let your hearts be troubled. You believe in God; believe also in me. *My Father's house has many rooms; if that were not so, would I have told you that I am going there to prepare a place for you?* *And if I go and prepare a place for you, I will come back and take you to be with me that you also may be where I am."*

My dear child, I know your heart is burdened by many things. This world is full of heart ache, disappointment, grief and uncertainty. There is a great darkness that seeks to overwhelm you, pointing you towards hopelessness and despair. Do not let your heart be troubled. No! Instead, curl up with me. Come to me. Let your belief in me, be your strength.

I have prepared a place for you. I have a place where you will know complete joy, peace, and love. This is my word to you.

It is an assured promise. This promise resides in my character and therefore, it is your hope.

As you long to know good, to experience life, to receive love, and grace, let your hope rest in me. Do not place this hope in any person, success or situation. Place your hope in my character. As you do so, your belief will increase, and you will know gratitude, even in the midst of today's troubles. Come to me, rest in me, abide in me and believe!

READING
150

What do
you hear?

LIVE

How will
you respond?

A prompt
for living

Do you know someone who is going through a troubling time? Take a moment to write a card to encourage them, point them towards Jesus, and remind them that they are not walking alone. Your friendship brings the light of Jesus.

LISTEN
John 14:4-6

⁴ "You know the way to the place where I am going." ⁵ Thomas said to him, "Lord, we don't know where you are going, so how can we know the way?" ⁶ Jesus answered, "I am the way and the truth and the life. No one comes to the Father except through me.

You search high and low for a way to experience life. I see you seek to find love and affection. I watch as you strive to earn your way through performance. I am a witness to your never-ending search for truth. I know that you are restless. I know that you can be filled with anxiety about how life will turn out. You turn and turn. You strive and toil. You weary yourself with remedies and temporary salvations.

My love, life is found in me and my Son is the only way to me. He came to you, I sent him to you out of great love for you. I sent him to you so that you would have a visual of the way of truth that leads to life.

Take a moment. Breathe in and think of your life. Do you feel the conflict within you? Do you know strife?

Do you feel the tiresome lengths you go to, to make life an abundant experience? Breathe again. Soak in the fact that I deeply love you. I rejoice over you. I delight in you. I long for what is good and right and perfect for you. It is my greatest desire for you to know life intimately. For when you know life, you know me.

Cease your striving, believe in my Son. He is truth. He is life. He is the way. Turn to him. Turn from self salvation to salvation that is given. Turn from your constant labor, hiding, apathy, and angst and ask my Son to reveal himself, his truth, his life and his way. Turn to him. He will lift you up and set you on solid ground. His love will pave the way to me. His love will give you freedom. His love is life.

.

**What do
you hear?**

LIVE

**How will
you respond?**

**A prompt
for living**

Take a moment and think of a person in your life who is striving. Perhaps a colleague? a friend? a loved one? Buy them a small and undeserved gift. Include a card with the gift explaining how you are praying they will know peace, life, and truth.

LISTEN
John 14:7-10

7 "If you really know me, you will know my Father as well. From now on, you do know him and have seen him." 8 Philip said, "Lord, show us the Father and that will be enough for us." 9 Jesus answered: "Don't you know me, Philip, even after I have been among you such a long time? Anyone who has seen me has seen the Father. How can you say, 'Show us the Father'? 10 Don't you believe that I am in the Father, and that the Father is in me? The words I say to you I do not speak on my own authority. Rather, it is the Father, living in me, who is doing his work.

I sent my Son that you might see a picture of me. I sent him so that you would know my heart for you and hear what I long for you to know. I sent him so that you would see my everlasting, deep and abiding love in the flesh. I sent him to identify with you. I sent him to suffer among you. I sent him to show you my heart.

What do you hear?

You look for me and at times you look past my Son; forgetting that he is in me and I am in him. You wonder where I am and what I think, yet you turn to countless other sources before looking to my Son. He is in me and I am in him. When you see him, you see me. This is a fact that will never change.

LIVE

When you wonder what I think of you, read the words of my Son.

When you question how work, look to my Son.

How will you respond?

When you long for truth to be revealed, go to my Son.

When you want to know my heart, root in my Son.

When you desire to be close with me, spend time in the story of my Son.

A prompt for living

He is in me and I am in him. Go to him. Turn to him. Root in him. Listen to him. Run, leap, and jump your way to him. As you know him, you will know me.

For one month, read a gospel a week. When there is a word, phrase, or concept that sticks out to you, write it down. When there is a story that moves you, tell someone. When there is a question that arises, ask it. Live in the story of Jesus for one month and let it shape your conversations with those you know.

READING
152

LISTEN
John 14:11

11 Believe me when I say that I am in the Father and the Father is in me; or at least believe on the evidence of the works themselves.

The earth declares my handiwork. The sun rises and falls scattering color across the canvas of the sky. Water flows, tumbling, dancing, moving, and creating roadways for life below its surface. The rain falls by my command, feeding the earth and renewing that which is dry. I direct each movement. I designed every part. I know it intimately and every element from the smallest flower to vast galaxies, perform their role giving glory to me with each moment.

The works of my hands are evidenced in my creation.

You too experience the works of my hands as you breathe and air fills your lungs. The very fact that blood flows through you, carrying nutrients to every part of your body is evidence of my work. When your needs are met and your body heals, my work is seen. My works are there to reveal me.

I have created the earth to prompt and increase belief.

Look to the works of my hands and believe.

Do the hard work of belief. Work it out in every part of your life. Turn to my Son, your belief in him, is belief in me. Your belief matters and that, my child, is why the entire earth functions with precise beauty, drawing every person, everywhere to believe in me. Believe my dear child. It truly is your greatest work.

**What do
you hear?**

LIVE

**How will
you respond?**

**A prompt
for living**

Go on a walk with a friend and simply point out the beauty surrounding you.

LISTEN
John 14:12-14

12 Very truly I tell you, whoever believes in me will do the works I have been doing, and they will do even greater things than these, because I am going to the Father. 13 And I will do whatever you ask in my name, so that the Father may be glorified in the Son. 14 You may ask me for anything in my name, and I will do it.

You often limit yourself. You think my vision for you is small and the plans I have for you comfortable. Do not hesitate to ask me for what I desire for you. Do not hesitate to dream and expect the impossible. I am the God who stopped the flow of the river Jordan, who opened the Red Sea, who sent manna from heaven and who rescued his people over and over again. I was glorified through my Son as he healed the sick, raised the dead, caused the lame to walk and gave the blind their sight. My son softens hardened hearts and open the eyes of the spiritually blind.

What do you hear?

Reading

154

When you come to me, in the name of my Son, you are coming to me in belief that I am not limited in any fashion. I desire to be glorified in your life and in your belief in my Son. Believe! Come to me and ask whatever you wish in the name of my Son Jesus. He will answer you. He will increase your belief. Do not limit me by asking for the possible. Trust me for the impossible. Your belief matters to me. Your requests of me are evidence of your belief in me.

LIVE

Come to me with your pain, dreams, desires, needs, ideas, and plans. Ask in the name of my Son, for my glory and watch. Watch for answers. Look for the impossible, making its way to the possible. Keep asking! With every ask your faith deepened and dependence in me is strengthened. Every time you ask, you choose to place your hope in my character and not in the fulfillment of a wish.

How will you respond?

A prompt for living

Is there something in your life that you have stopped praying for, for you have not seen it answered? Go again to God in the name of Jesus and ask. Ask that your belief would be increased and that you want to believe that He will answer you.

LISTEN
John 14:15

15 "If you love me, keep my commands."

Beloved, I am not a cruel god who wishes for you to follow a set of rules to show off my power. I do not need your obedience to justify myself. I do not need your obedience to prove that I am god. Your obedience is not for me, it is for you.

When you are obedient you reveal your trust in me as the Creator of life. Your obedience is the face of your trust. It is the evidence that you believe I created life and I know how it is best experienced. Trust and obedience are intimately tied. You cannot have one without the other.

If you obey but do not trust, you will not know freedom. You will live in a bondage that leads toward legalistic practices.

If you say you trust me, but do not obey, you are fooling yourself. Trust evidences itself in behavior.

My beloved, trust and obey. Trust that my love for you is deep. Trust that I am good and right and perfect and desire for you what is good and right and perfect. Trust that I know the workings of life intimately. Trust that I am for you. Trust that I desire your freedom.

Trust in me and live. Let your life shine before all people allowing your obedience to speak of my ways and my kingdom. Let you life declare your trust in my character. Let your life reveal your love for me, which in turn displays my complete love for you.

Oh I long for you to know and walk with me in obedience. It is a joy to see my children choose to trust me with their lives. I delight in your trust. I am thankful for your obedience. I rejoice in your freedom.

What do you hear?

LIVE

How will you respond?

A prompt for living

Do you know the good you are to do? Is there an idea that keeps popping into your mind? Is there a step you feel motivated to take? Have you been putting off some good thing for a lesser thing? If so, confess your hesitation and jump in! Obey the prompting of your heart and do the good you were told!

LISTEN
John 14:16-17

16 And I will ask the Father, and he will give you another advocate to help you and be with you forever—17 the Spirit of truth. The world cannot accept him, because it neither sees him nor knows him. But you know him, for he lives with you and will be in you.

You long for truth. I know, you ask for it often. I observe your search for truth. I hear your cries to believe what is good. You struggle to believe truth. It is much more tempting for you to live in deception. You have an enemy and his name is liar. He seeks to destroy you. Through lies he convinces you that you are not valuable. He somehow has convinced you that you are too much or you are not enough. He twists and turns words into thoughts that kill your soul. He is a voice you've come to know and unfortunately, his voice is a voice you've chosen to believe.

I have given you a Spirit of truth, MY Spirit. My Spirit speaks only that which leads to life. My Spirit speaks only that which is true. My Spirit is consistent, full of grace, abounding in love, and will always speak with wisdom and invite you to believe.

The voice of the liar is loud in your mind and you've made agreements with him in your heart. My Spirit, the Spirit of truth, is gentle, and kind to you, and will with one whisper wipe out the lies of your enemy. I long for you to believe my voice, through my Spirit and believe what I say is truth.

My beloved, come to me with your thoughts. Speak aloud the thoughts that tell you, you must control, you are shameful, you are not valuable, you must earn forgiveness. Speak aloud the thoughts telling you that I don't care, that I'm not real, or too busy. Speak aloud the thoughts that cause fear, anxiety, shame, and worry. When you speak these lies aloud, confess them as such and ask my Spirit to fill you with the Spirit of truth.

My Spirit will bring truth to you. My Spirit will whisper life into your soul and your Spirit will be met with mine and live in life and truth. Turn from the lies of the enemy and cling to the words of truth, given to you by my Spirit.

What do you hear?

LIVE

How will you respond?

A prompt for living

Do you know a friend who is trapped in a lie? Sometime this week, intentionally speak truth over them and pray that the lies they believe would be replaced by the words of truth and that they would know, deep within them, the Spirit of truth.

LISTEN
John 14:18-21

18 I will not leave you as orphans; I will come to you. 19 Before long, the world will not see me anymore, but you will see me. Because I live, you also will live. 20 On that day you will realize that I am in my Father, and you are in me, and I am in you. 21 Whoever has my commands and keeps them is the one who loves me. The one who loves me will be loved by my Father, and I too will love them and show myself to them."

What do you hear?

You are accustomed to people leaving you. You've grown familiar with feelings of abandonment. You are acquainted with loneliness. I know in this world you have experienced the pain of rejection and the heart ache of being used and forgotten. These experiences grieve me. These feelings are not a part of my way.

My son is in me and you are found in my Son. Therefore, you are in me. I will never leave you nor will I forsake you. I will not abandon you to evil or take you to the depths to leave you there alone. I will not use you for my sake and drop you as though you're no longer useful to me. I am constant. I am present always. I am with you, even until the very end of the age.

My love for you is much deeper than the love of any human. You can be free in my love, for my love and the gift of my presence are not tied to performance or to behavior of any kind. My love and presence are gifts that are given without condition and are permanent fixtures in your life. These words are true.

When you feel the sting of rejection on earth, come to me. When you feel abandoned, turn to me. When you know loneliness, lean into me. I am your home. I am your most constant companion. I am your very source of life, love, and presence. My beloved, walk freely in these words, knowing they are not empty thoughts, but the actual reality of being in found my Son and my Son in me.

LIVE

How will you respond?

A prompt for living

Take time to serve an abandoned people group by giving your presence to them. Do not give a donation, write a letter or send a gift. Instead, give yourself, let your eyes see those which know the sting of rejection and love them through relationship.

READING
157

LISTEN
John 14:22-24

22 Then Judas (not Judas Iscariot) said, "But, Lord, why do you intend to show yourself to us and not to the world?" 23 Jesus replied, "Anyone who loves me will obey my teaching. My Father will love them, and we will come to them and make our home with them. 24 Anyone who does not love me will not obey my teaching. These words you hear are not my own; they belong to the Father who sent me.

READING

158

I know that there are things you do not understand. I know that my ways at times do not seem right or just. This is evidenced by your questions of me. You know how the world works from a finite perspective. You ask why I don't reveal myself to every person, without realizing that I revealed myself completely in my Son. I love the world so very much, the entire world. I gave my one and only Son; that whomever believes in him would never experience separation from me, but they would instead experience eternal life with me.

When you believe in my Son, you make your home with us. You place your tent in our camp and you belong to our family. My family is grand and full and rich and good. You take on the family name and you inherit the traits of my family. My Spirit gives you love, joy, peace, patience, kindness, goodness, gentleness, and self-control. These are the character traits of my family. There is no law forbidding any of them. Every character trait I give, leads to life. Every single one!

My beloved child, you are a part of a royal family. Your obedience counts. Your obedience is proof of belief and your acceptance of my love. Everything I ask of you is out of good and love for you. Trust in this. Trust that I am a good Father. Trust in my Son, whom I gave out of abundant love for you. Join us, dwell in my Spirit, let him live through you. Let your life speak of the family to whom you belong.

What do you hear?

LIVE

How will you respond?

A prompt for living

When you receive a cold call or interact with a rude sales associate, respond to them with grace. Ask them how their day is? Use your brief interaction with these individuals to bless them, extend grace, show love, and ooze the character of your Father!

LISTEN
John 14:25-27

* "All this I have spoken while still with you. ²⁶ But the Advocate, the Holy Spirit, whom the Father will send in my name, will teach you all things and will remind you of everything I have said to you. ²⁷ Peace I leave with you; my peace I give you. I do not give to you as the world gives. Do not let your hearts be troubled and do not be afraid.*

The ache of your heart is real. In this world you will have trouble. I however am not of this world, I have overcome the world. I know you fear returning to hurt. I know there is risk when you step out. I see the pain that you once experienced and how that pain is your muscle memory creating fear and anxiety. I know that you have experienced tragedy and loss. I grieve and weep with the broken hearted. I grieve and weep with you. Your pain does not fall on blind eyes or a cold heart.

There is no circumstance in your life where you walk alone. I sent my Spirit to you as your constant companion. When you walk through the valley of the shadow of death, there is no need to fear evil, for my Spirit is with you. He is your protection and footing. Place your trust again in me. I am your hope. I am the one who holds your heart. I am the one who will lead you to places, which I fully intend to take you. I will never play with your heart, nor will I abandon you to despair. I will never leave a gaping hole in need of provision. My name is healer. My name is Life. My name is Provider.

As you walk through the circumstances of this day, do not fear. I have not abandoned you. You are in the middle. You are in the space between need and provision. You are in the space between risk and reward. You are in the place between despair and restoration. You are in the middle. The middle is the darkest place. It is the place where my Spirit is needed to sustain you, to give you hope, and to increase your faith. In the middle my Spirit is needed to be your constant companion and to be the lamp unto your feet and the light unto your path. My Spirit is the guide through the middle. He will walk with you every step of the journey. Lean into him. Trust his leading. Let him be your source of hope, comfort, joy, protection, provision, and peace. Be not afraid, when you face troubles of many kinds. Remember, I am good and this darkness overwhelming you is not beyond my care.

What do you hear?

LIVE

How will you respond?

A prompt for living

Are you experiencing darkness? Fear? Need? Tell someone and pray with them for your faith to increase and for you to know peace. Turn from fear and walk toward truth. Do you know someone who is struggling with fear? Send this word to them and remind them that they do not walk alone.

LISTEN
John 14:28-31

28 "You heard me say, 'I am going away and I am coming back to you.' If you loved me, you would be glad that I am going to the Father, for the Father is greater than I. 29 I have told you now before it happens, so that when it does happen you will believe. 30 I will not say much more to you, for the prince of this world is coming. He has no hold over me, 31 but he comes so that the world may learn that I love the Father and do exactly what my Father has commanded me. "Come now; let us leave.

I am greater. These words need to be ingrained into your heart, mind, soul, body, and spirit. I am greater.

Your heart worries. I am greater.
You fear the events of the days ahead. I am greater.
You think you'll never get out of your current situation. I am greater.
You feel lonely. I am greater.
You feel unwanted. I am greater.
You lack provision. I am greater.
Your vision is grand. I am greater.
Your dreams are big. I am greater.
Your spirit is troubled. I am greater.

Your body is tired. I am greater.
Your hope is wavering. I am greater.
You're in over your head. I am greater.
You need help. I am greater.
You feel empty. I am greater.
You've also known joy. I am greater still.
You've known miracles. I am greater still.
You've known delight. I am greater still.
You've known peace, kindness, and truth. I am greater still.

I am greater than the most precious good you've known and the deepest sorrow you've tasted. I am greater. Let this be your hope no matter your circumstance. I am greater.

What do you hear?

LIVE

How will you respond?

A prompt for living

Today, listen intently to the words of those around you. When you hear words of celebration, celebrate with those who speak and encourage them. When you hear words of sorrow or worry, weep with them. Let them know that you've heard and encourage them. In practical ways encourage those around you to know the God is greater than celebrations and sorrow. Be a practical example of grace.

John 15   (Readings 161–168)

¹ "I am the true vine, and my Father is the gardener. ² He cuts off every branch in me that bears no fruit, while every branch that does bear fruit he prunes so that it will be even more fruitful.

I care about the fruit of your life. It is valuable to me. The fruit of your life is the evidence of your root system and also my love for you.

When I cut off branches that are growing wildly or are unhealthy, I am loving you. When I cut off branches simply because you have too much going on and the sheer amount of branches you have cannot be sustained, I am loving you. When I cut off branches that are healthy, so that they'll grow with greater strength, I am loving you. When I prune your life, I am loving you.

I know pruning is painful. Pruning, to the inattentive heart can feel like punishment or cruelty, for it is painful. But I am not cruel. I prune out of love and deep care and pruning is always for your good. Your life will bear more fruit, good fruit, as I cut off that which will steal from your life or inhibit growth.

When it feels as though you are being shaped or stripped in some way, ask me to show you what I'm doing. Ask me to show you where I'm working in you. When the pain of pruning is felt, pray for belief. Pray for increased trust and welcome me as the gardener of your life.

READING
161

**What do
you hear?**

LIVE

**How will
you respond?**

**A prompt
for living**

If you live near a winery, grab a friend who is going through a season of being pruned and allow your surroundings to be an encouraging metaphor. If you do not, grab a bottle of wine and a few friends and talk about a time in life where you now know you were being pruned. Encourage one another with your stories.

LISTEN
John 15:3-4

³ You are already clean because of the word I have spoken to you. ⁴ Remain in me, as I also remain in you. No branch can bear fruit by itself; it must remain in the vine. Neither can you bear fruit unless you remain in me.

It is truth, that a branch that is not connected to a vine is dead. It is of no use, except to be used as firewood. All branches must be connected to the vine, to a tree, to the stem, to the stalk, every branch no matter how big must remain in a life source.

I am your life source. Therefore, remain, take root in, make your home in, me.

I know that at times the word pictures I paint are difficult to understand. I know that you want a straight answer, a formula. I however am bigger than formulas. I'm larger than a simple answer. Word pictures paint the most accurate way of relating to me. This picture holds deep truth for you. You must learn to remain in me. You must gain your identity from me. You must be given your value from me. For apart from me you swim from here to there trying to obtain value as best you can. You try to fit your branch into other life sources. But when you seek to connect your branch to something other than me, it is as though you are a tree branch seeking to obtain life through a dead corn stalk, it simply will never work.

When you remain in me, you are choosing to identify with me, find your identity as my child and live in the complete value that I give. This value can never be earned and therefore can never be taken away. My beloved, it is my desire that you have life, abundant and full, this can only happen when you are attached to me, the true vine.

What do
you hear?

LIVE

How will
you respond?

A prompt
for living

Gather a few friends together and ask them from where they obtain their identity. Talk about Jesus as the true source of identity. What are the ramifications of identity found and lived in Jesus versus identity found and lived in others, things, and activities?

LISTEN
John 15:5-8

[5] *"I am the vine; you are the branches. If you remain in me and I in you, you will bear much fruit; apart from me you can do nothing. [6] If you do not remain in me, you are like a branch that is thrown away and withers; such branches are picked up, thrown into the fire and burned. [7] If you remain in me and my words remain in you, ask whatever you wish, and it will be done for you. [8] This is to my Father's glory, that you bear much fruit, showing yourselves to be my disciples.*

My beloved, mine is the way of life. My son invites you to take up root in him, my Son and I are one, therefore, by taking root in him, you root also in me. Where you find your life source is an important matter. Take your nutrients from me, and my words for you.

Mine is the way of hope. Derive your hope from me. Mine is the way of love. Soak up the love of my fertile soil and allow it to richly feed you. Mine is the way of truth. Surround yourself with my words, letting them give to your life, forming you, and teaching you. Oh my beloved, it is kindness that invites you to take up root in me and my Son. Let my kindness richly form you. Let my kindness lead you away from false sources and lead you to the way of life.

When you take up root in me, my life, my hope, my love, and my truth your life will bear the fruit of my Spirit. The world around you will see that you follow a way not of this world. They will question you and wonder from where it is that you have learned to live. They will see light in you. They will see my hope springing up from you in the midst of the most challenging circumstances. They will see me.

It is good that others see me in you, for you are my ambassador. You represent me as you walk through each day. Your life takes on the characteristics of my life, as you remain in me, as you root yourself in me. It is a glorious thing, when I your Father, see the fruit of your life as you remain in me. My heart aches for your life to know this truth with your whole being. Root yourself in me. Plant yourself in the rich soil of my life and remain in me. For apart from me, you can literally do nothing.

What do you hear?

LIVE

How will you respond?

A prompt for living

As you walk today look around you at the vegetation. What do you see? What do you notice? Can you tell what kind of plant it is by its leaves, color and fruit? Ask Jesus to reveal his way to you. When you have a thought to remember a friend, call someone, encourage someone, smile at someone, go visit someone, perform a random act of kindness, give a gift, or simply look someone in the eye. Do not hesitate, follow your thought with action. Watch as you follow these promptings, how the fruit of life is shown as you live out the good grown in you through a root system in Jesus.

LISTEN
John 15:9

⁹ *"As the Father has loved me, so have I loved you. Now remain in my love."*

Love is a concept that is foreign and longed for by most in this world. It is what you were created by. Love is what you were created for. Love is the most beautiful and powerful ideal and action any person can live into or experience. Love is not the same as enjoyment, though you often use it as such. Love instead is a deep reality of complete acceptance. It breathes life. Love gives hope. Love speaks truth with gentleness and respect. Love sits with. Love waits for. Love is gracious and kind. Love is generous. Love is simple. And, love is incredibly profound.

Love is not a feeling, though you can feel it. Love is not an emotion, though it evokes emotion. Love is not based on opinion, but complete acceptance. Love is truth. Love is expressed in joy. Love is a gift. Love is always a gift. Love,

when given, is about the one to whom it is give. Love is does not demand love in return. Love invites to love. Love sets free. Love binds up broken pieces. Love makes beautiful things from ashes. Love comforts those who mourn. Love proclaims good. Love doesn't see social standing. Love releases prisoners from darkness. Love invites you to life. Love is complete.

Love can be experienced. Love can be given. Love can be received. Love can be denied. But love, the kind of love I give, will never fail. Soak in my love. Sit back into my love and let it overwhelm you. Let my love seep into your lungs and fill you with life and light. Let my love be your source. Let my love be your hope. Let my love be your everlasting joy.

Remain in my love. Remain in me.

Reading
164

**What do
you hear?**

LIVE

**How will
you respond?**

**A prompt
for living**

Pray for your neighbors by name. Ask Jesus to show you a way that you can practically love them. Perhaps you can serve them in some way. Maybe it's cooking for them or simply meeting them. Maybe the beginning of showing love is simply knowing your neighbors' names. Love with action, generosity, and selflessness.

LISTEN
John 15:10-13

If you keep my commands, you will remain in my love, just as I have kept my Father's commands and remain in his love. ¹¹ I have told you this so that my joy may be in you and that your joy may be complete. ¹² My command is this: Love each other as I have loved you. ¹³ Greater love has no one than this: to lay down one's life for one's friends."

You do not naturally lay your life down. It is not within you to do so on your own accord. It is my love living through you that enables you to lay aside self for the sake of another. This is the way of love.

There is no greater love, than one who lays down his own life for the life of a friend. My son gave his life up for you. He put aside his rights, his attributes, his royalty, and ultimately his human life out of love. His joy was complete.

My love for you is deep and enables you to live a life of love and sacrifice much like my Son's. My love breathes life into you and gives you the ability to step aside to let another be seen.

My love is not human. It does not come with condition. You too can love this way as you remain in me. This is the greatest command, for when you remain in perfect love, you are able to give love that is steeped in joy and sacrifice. This is the kind of love that humans long for and do not understand. This is the kind of love that sets prisoners free. This is the kind of love that heals and makes beauty from ashes. When one loves by laying down rights, time, position, and even one's own life, I am seen, for this love is not natural.

Lay down your life my child. When you do, you will know a complete joy and you will show a watching world a glimpse of me.

READING
165

What do
you hear?

LIVE

How will
you respond?

A prompt
for living

Are there things on your to do list that are getting in the way of relationship with someone? Go through your schedule and see what you might be able to lay down, so that you might be able to love someone else with your time.

LISTEN
John 15:14-16

14 "You are my friends if you do what I command. 15 I no longer call you servants, because a servant does not know his master's business. Instead, I have called you friends, for everything that I learned from my Father I have made known to you."

Friendship is a sacred relationship. It is a union of trust between two people. Friendship is a huge value of my kingdom. I have taught my Son, and he shares all he knows with you. You are not a subservient. You are in fact a friend. You are a member of a great fellowship. You are a part of my kingdom! Friendship is the avenue by which I choose to grow my kingdom around the world.

When you trust that you are a friend of Jesus, my Son, you serve and give and love out of a trusted relationship. It is not your responsibility to earn anything from me. For that is impossible. It is yours to receive and to give, as in any trusted relationship.

Trust the words my Son has spoken to you are true. Trust that he does not want your guilt based service, for you are in fact a friend. True friends do not earn from one another. True friends trust that the relationship is good and right and that every act of service is performed out of love for the other.

When you serve out of love, you serve with pure motive and true friendship.

My beloved, receive from Jesus the friendship he offers. Receive from him and give out of relationship, rather than for it (which you often do). Trust in these words and live out of the truth they hold.

**What do
you hear?**

LIVE

**How will
you respond?**

**A prompt
for living**

Take time to write 5 cards this week and tell your friends what they mean to you and encourage them with your thoughts on your friendship and what you've learned from your friendship with Jesus.

16 "You did not choose me, but I chose you and appointed you so that you might go and bear fruit—fruit that will last—and so that whatever you ask in my name the Father will give you. 17 This is my command: Love each other."

You did not choose me. No my child, I chose you. I created you and chose every part of you. I chose for your heart to work in the way it does. I chose to give you the eyes that see the things your eyes see. I chose for your ears to hear what they do. I chose for you have a mind that processes things a very particular way. I chose your body. I chose your strengths and I chose your weaknesses. I chose to create you, and with great intention you were made.

I not only chose to make you as I did, I chose you to be with me. I chose for you to know me and to walk with me.

I chose you to be mine. This is a relationship like none other. Your entire role is to respond, never to earn, never to initiate, never to run, or chase after. You only respond to me and the only pure response to my choosing you is love. Love for me and love for the people around you. The fruit of your life is a result of your belief in my choosing you.

When you believe that I have chosen you, you live out of gratitude and you live a life that reflects my heart and my heart is always good and right and perfect and full of love.

Reading
167

What do you hear?

LIVE

How will you respond?

A prompt for living

When you interact with strangers today, whether on the road, in person, or on the phone see how you might be able to communicate value, give dignity, and show love. Make it your aim to respond to being chosen by God by choosing to love others.

18 "If the world hates you, keep in mind that it hated me first. 19 If you belonged to the world, it would love you as its own. As it is, you do not belong to the world, but I have chosen you out of the world. That is why the world hates you. 20 Remember what I told you: 'A servant is not greater than his master.' If they persecuted me, they will persecute you also. If they obeyed my teaching, they will obey yours also. 21 They will treat you this way because of my name, for they do not know the one who sent me. 22 If I had not come and spoken to them, they would not be guilty of sin; but now they have no excuse for their sin. 23 Whoever hates me hates my Father as well. 24 If I had not done among them the works no one else did, they would not be guilty of sin. As it is, they have seen, and yet they have hated both me and my Father. 25 But this is to fulfill what is written in their Law: 'They hated me without reason 26 "When the Advocate comes, whom I will send to you from the Father—the Spirit of truth who goes out from the Father—he will testify about me. 27 And you also must testify, for you have been with me from the beginning."

You know well the spirit of the adversary, he is the one who lies to you over and over. He is the one who wants you to believe the worst about yourself and others. His language is deception and his words, only lies.

You were not given the adversary, but I did give you an Advocate. I have given you a voice of truth. Whose language is always good and right and perfect. His language is always filled with life and leads you to life's very source. Your advocate goes before you. He prepares your way. He speaks to words from my very heart. Lean into Him.

He tells the story of my Son. He awakens people to his reality. He breathes life and gives hope. He is and always will be the very source of truth in your life.

My beloved, when a voice seeks to kill steal or destroy you with its words do not listen. When a thought leads you to depths of confusion, anxiety, and misbelieve, do not listen. When a whisper tells you I am a lie or that my Son was a fool, do not listen. These are the words of the enemy of your soul. Do not heed them. Do not give ownership to them. Turn and walk away.

Cling to that which is pure, noble, righteous, and life-giving. Listen to the words that speak what is best. Listen to the words that declare my heart and my truth. Listen to the words that encourage you to love, have patience, be kind, thoughtful, and generous. Listen to the words that tell you are a child of a great King. These words always come from my heart. I will sing them over you as long as you live.

**What do
you hear?**

LIVE

**How will
you respond?**

**A prompt
for living**

Today, speak life over a person in your life who is troubled. Ask Holy Spirit to speak to you and write a card or email encouraging this person and pointing them towards life.

JOHN 16 (Readings 169–176)

LISTEN
John 16:1–6

¹ "All this I have told you so that you will not fall away. ² They will put you out of the synagogue; in fact, the time is coming when anyone who kills you will think they are offering a service to God. ³ They will do such things because they have not known the Father or me. ⁴ I have told you this, so that when their time comes you will remember that I warned you about them. I did not tell you this from the beginning because I was with you, ⁵ but now I am going to him who sent me. None of you asks me, 'Where are you going?' ⁶ Rather, you are filled with grief because I have said these things."

I have prepared you for all things. I have forewarned you of coming troubles. I have set before you a path of righteousness and good that is beyond your current understanding. Much of my word does not make sense to you at your first hearing. You hear words of warning or blessing and glance over them as though they are not words from me.

Then, the day of trouble comes and you remember my words. You remember that I warned you of persecution. I spoke to you about the trouble you would experience for following after me. You will know the great sisterhood of joy and sorrow as you walk in your times of trouble. Your memory is key. Remember that I am with you. Remember that I am for you and your good. Listen to the words of my Son and remember them in your times of trial. Remember that he loved you so much that he prepared your way.

When you know my Son, you know me, your loving, caring, and generous Father. It is not my desire that you suffer, but it is my hope that you cling to me in the midst of it.

Reading
169

What do you hear?

LIVE

How will you respond?

A prompt for living

Do you know someone going through a difficult time? Take time today to give them courage through words!

LISTEN
John 16:7-11

7 "But very truly I tell you, it is for your good that I am going away. Unless I go away, the Advocate will not come to you; but if I go, I will send him to you. 8 When he comes, he will prove the world to be in the wrong about sin and righteousness and judgment: 9 about sin, because people do not believe in me; 10 about righteousness, because I am going to the Father, where you can see me no longer; 11 and about judgment, because the prince of this world now stands condemned."

Yes my child, my Spirit, your advocate has come. He comes so that you will know the truth of me and my work in the world. He will show you what is good. He will speak to you truth. He will show you a way that is right. A way that is truth. A way filled with belief.

My Spirit, your advocate, will whisper truth in your ear, against the lies of the enemy. He will always speak that which is right.

My beloved, seek to know his voice, for his voice, is mine. I long for you to know the truth of my love for you.

I long to tell you the deep things of my kingdom. I want to whisper great truths about your created way and how deeply I care for you. These words are often muted by the shouts of the enemy, the prince of this world who wants nothing more for you than for you to believe lies about my Son, about me, about you.

Seek my voice! Seek the one who will always tell you what is truth, the one whose words will bring life to your soul and calm your spirit. Seek my voice. Listen closely. I am here, I am speaking . . . listen and live.

What do you hear?

LIVE

How will you respond?

A prompt for living

Today make a conscious decision to speak only words that are kind and life-giving at all times. When someone complains, choose to speak words of kindness. When someone gossips, choose to speak life over the person being talked about. When someone cuts you off on the freeway, ask God to get them to their destination safely and give them peace if there are things in life causing hurry.

LISTEN
John 16:12-15

12 "I have much more to say to you, more than you can now bear. 13 But when he, the Spirit of truth, comes, he will guide you into all the truth. He will not speak on his own; he will speak only what he hears, and he will tell you what is yet to come. 14 He will glorify me because it is from me that he will receive what he will make known to you. 15 All that belongs to the Father is mine. That is why I said the Spirit will receive from me what he will make known to you."

The situation you are in needs my leading. I understand it is outside of your knowledge and mind to comprehend all that is taking place. I also know that you need wisdom, guidance, and truth. Truth comes only from one source, me. I am truth. My son is in me and he is the truth as well. His Spirit, which was given to you, is the very Spirit of truth.

When life is overwhelming and wisdom is needed, seek truth. Listen for truth. Do not seek the opinions of man, for the wisdom of man is foolishness to me. Do not go from person to person to find the best answer to your dilemma. Do not seek to reason your way out of your situation.

Come to me. Listen for the Spirit of truth to give you all wisdom, knowledge, and understanding.

My Spirit of truth will lead you. You must trust obey his leading. Even though the truth may lead you in a way that holds no common sense and is not reasonable, my truth will always lead you to life. My son, his very truth is the way to life. The three are tied together; one always builds and leads to the other. Therefore, when you hear a whisper of truth, inviting you to live in a certain way, you can guarantee that way will lead you to life.

What do you hear?

LIVE

How will you respond?

A prompt for living

Is there a situation in your life that you are needing wisdom? Have you asked for the opinion of many others? Take time to pray, ask Holy Spirit what you should do. Ask three friends to pray with you. Together, listen for Holy Spirit to speak. What scriptures, thoughts, or ideas come to mind? Get together with your three friends and discuss what you heard, thought, or envisioned. If something stands out as a way to walk in, choose to be obedient.

LISTEN
John 16:16–18

16 Jesus went on to say, "In a little while you will see me no more, and then after a little while you will see me." 17 At this, some of his disciples said to one another, "What does he mean by saying, 'In a little while you will see me no more, and then after a little while you will see me,' and 'Because I am going to the Father'?" 18 They kept asking, "What does he mean by 'a little while'? We don't understand what he is saying."

For you, there is mystery to me. There are many things about my ways that you do not understand, nor will you until they have come and gone. It is not yours to understand, but it is yours to trust. I know this past week your life has held with it the mysterious. I know that there are situations you do not understand. I know that you do know my ways. I know that you search for meaning and find none.

Trust in me.

I know that you desire to walk in faithfulness. I know that you think it would be easier to follow me if you knew every detail of what I was about in your life today. Trust is important. Trust that I know what is best. Trust that I am doing good in your story and even that which feels difficult is a part of my story for you. I am working all things together for your good. I am working all things together for the good of those around you.

Today, as you face trials of many kinds, and today, as you experience unexpected joys, trust me. Trust that I am bringing about good. Trust that I am doing more than you can imagine and continue to walk with me in obedience.

Trust in me my beloved. Trust and walk, for with me, good is your constant companion.

What do you hear?

LIVE

How will you respond?

A prompt for living

Next time you go to a worship gathering, pray and ask God to use you to encourage someone. When you go to sit, intentionally sit next to someone you do not know. Remind that person, at some point during the gathering that God is with them and remind them that God is for them. Encourage them with the hope you have.

LISTEN
John 16:19-22

19 Jesus saw that they wanted to ask him about this, so he said to them, "Are you asking one another what I meant when I said, 'In a little while you will see me no more, and then after a little while you will see me'? 20 Very truly I tell you, you will weep and mourn while the world rejoices. You will grieve, but your grief will turn to joy. 21 A woman giving birth to a child has pain because her time has come; but when her baby is born she forgets the anguish because of her joy that a child is born into the world. 22 So with you: Now is your time of grief, but I will see you again and you will rejoice, and no one will take away your joy."

Wait my child. Your time has not yet come. You place your hope in the things of this world and that hope is often crushed. Place your hope in me. My timing is perfect. My ways are beyond your understanding.

Trust me in your time of trial. Trust that I will bring good to you. Trust that I will see you through. Trust that you will not be abandoned or left alone. It is good for you to walk through the valley of the shadow of death. When you do, you grow to know my presence in the midst of trial. When you face trials and difficulties, you grow in faith and belief. When you persevere you come to know hope. Walk in this hope, this hope is from me and is set on eternal things. This hope will turn your mourning into dancing and the trials you once faced with anguish, disappear to a memory.

A memory, which now brings you hope and peace. A memory, which increases belief and deepens faith. My beloved, though you do not understand, keep walking, and believe that I am bringing about good for you!

Reading

173

What do you hear?

LIVE

How will you respond?

A prompt for living

Make a point to give away courage during your day. When someone voices self-doubt, speak words of truth over them, when someone voices uncertainty, speak hope, when someone speaks of darkness, speak of light. Use your words with those around you to give away courage.

LISTEN
John 16:23-24

It is my desire to complete your joy. It is not mine to strip joy from those I love. I know that my ways are not your ways and in fact sometimes the way I go about increasing and completing your joy, may actually, in the moment, feel as though it's being decreased.

Trust that my plans are greater than yours. Trust and watch. Believe and hope. I am who I am. I am truth. I am complete joy. I am love. These define me. Therefore, every gift I bring to you will be complete and will not be lacking in anything.

When it feels as though you are losing hope. Ask me and I will be your hope. When you feel disappointed, ask me, and I will come through. I am a perfect loving Father and I desire good for my children. If you were to ask your closest friend or most loving family member for bread, would they give you a hand full of nails? No, of course not. Then you can expect more from me, for I am perfect.

Come to me with your requests. Approach me with boldness. Tell me what it is that you want, and thank me in advance for my care and provision. The question is never, can I accomplish what you ask. When you think this, you question me. However, I do know what is best for you and will give you what you ask as you trust in me and what you ask is for your good.

I will never give you that which will harm you—that is outside of my character. Approach me with boldness and reverence. I, your loving Father will hear you and will answer.

What do you hear?

LIVE

How will you respond?

A prompt for living

Pray today for someone in your life who is experiencing difficulty. Ask boldly of God, your Father, in the name of Jesus. Make a commitment to pray for good for this person, and let them know you are praying.

LISTEN
John 16:25-28

25 "Though I have been speaking figuratively, a time is coming when I will no longer use this kind of language but will tell you plainly about my Father. 26 In that day you will ask in my name. I am not saying that I will ask the Father on your behalf. 27 No, the Father himself loves you because you have loved me and have believed that I came from God. 28 I came from the Father and entered the world; now I am leaving the world and going back to the Father."

When you love my Son and believe in his name, you love me. Your love and trust in my Son, is love and trust in me. Oh, it is not your work for me that I long for. It is not what you accomplish, for me that makes me glad. It is not your performance, your masterful ability to obey the law, it's not your morality or your human actions that speak of your love for me. No, these are all works of your hand and are all noise to me without love. It is crucial. It is imperative that you love my Son, that you believe in him and that you love me.

Like a good earthly father, when you trust my love for you, it is the most precious gift to me. When you believe in my Son, you also believe in me. You declare your love for me. Just like a human lover, the greatest gift you can bring them is your trust in their love and your love in return, I your heavenly Father want nothing more than for you to believe and love.

My love for you is so vast. It is wide. It is deep. It is long. It is powerful. Come to me with boldness in prayer for your boldness is your way of showing you trust in my Son and receive my love. My beloved child, give me the gift of belief. Give me the gift of trust. Give me the gift of receiving my love and then love me out of that love I've given you.

READING

175

What do
you hear?

LIVE

How will
you respond?

A prompt
for living

Write a letter to your parents and tell them that you love them. If these seems impossible, ask Jesus to fill you with his love and give you his perspective on your family. Take a risk and speak words of love to your family, to your parents, and let them know this is possible because of God's great love for you.

LISTEN
John 16:29-33

29 Then Jesus' disciples said, "Now you are speaking clearly and without figures of speech. 30 Now we can see that you know all things and that you do not even need to have anyone ask you questions. This makes us believe that you came from God." 31 "Do you now believe?" Jesus replied. 32 "A time is coming and in fact has come when you will be scattered, each to your own home. You will leave me all alone. Yet I am not alone, for my Father is with me. 33 "I have told you these things, so that in me you may have peace. In this world you will have trouble. But take heart! I have overcome the world."

Take heart! I have overcome the world. The darkness you feel, I am the light. The death you're grieving, I am the light. The lack you know, I am provider. The emptiness you know, I am your purpose. The hopelessness you know, I am hope. The condemnation you've experienced, I am grace. The loneliness you know, I am a friend. The hatred you've felt, I am love. The judgment you've known, I am mercy.

Take heart. I have overcome this dark world. Though at this time, you experience the dark, you can know light in my Son.

Though in this world you will have trouble, you need not be overwhelmed by it, for I, your God, have overcome the darkness of this world. Trust that this is true. Trust that I am for your good in all things and that I work all things together for your good. Trust that when you walk through the valley of the shadow of death there is no need to fear evil, I am with you. I am for you. I am your strength and your footing.

Take heart. Have courage. I am for you. I am with you.

Reading
176

What do you hear?

LIVE

How will you respond?

A prompt for living

Buy a candle for a friend going through a dark time. Write a card to give with the candle describing how light always overwhelms the darkness and snuffs it out. Encourage them to light the candle when they are feeling overwhelmed to remind themselves that Jesus is the light and light will always win.

JOHN 17 (Readings 177–183)

LISTEN
John 17:1

¹ Jesus spoke these things; and lifting up His eyes to heaven, He said, "Father, the hour has come; glorify Your Son, that the Son may glorify You . . ."

I know the plans you have, and the visions I've given seem far off. I know that you wonder why they've not come to fruition in your time. I know that you want to live into the visions and dreams that I've placed within you. Trust. Have patience. Even my son had to wait for the right time. It is important that you listen to me. Trust that I am holding every part of your life.

My timing is always perfect. I will always accomplish that which I've placed in you. I will always do my good through you. I will do it at the exact right time, for it would go against my character to do so in any other way. Your timing is based on your outlook and your life circumstances.

Your timing only keeps you and your idea of what others need around you in mind. My timing weaves together the entire world. I will accomplish my will through you, in a manner that will bring me the most glory. I will glorify myself through you. I will bring you to the place of impossibility and I will reveal myself through you there.

When you grow weary of waiting. When you feel put on hold. When you question and cry, come to me, and I will renew your strength. This time of waiting increases your faith, enlarges your vision, and readies those around you. Trust in me. Walk with me. And, believe that I am about a good thing, in perfect time.

READING
177

What do you hear?

LIVE

How will you respond?

A prompt for living

Do you know someone who is confused about what to do with life? Someone who is discouraged as they wait? Make a point to take some time to pray for them and ask if you can take them out for coffee, or if their far away, set up a Skype/phone date. When you meet together, ask them what is on their mind and listen, and encourage.

LISTEN
John 17:1-5

¹ Jesus spoke these things; and lifting up His eyes to heaven, He said, "Father, the hour has come; glorify Your Son, that the Son may glorify You, ² even as You gave Him authority over all flesh, that to all whom You have given Him, He may give eternal life. ³ This is eternal life, that they may know You, the only true God, and Jesus Christ whom You have sent. ⁴ I glorified You on the earth, having accomplished the work which You have given Me to do. ⁵ Now, Father, glorify Me together with Yourself, with the glory which I had with You before the world was."

It's difficult to explain in words that you will understand the entirety of the work I did through my Son. He came and I revealed my glory through him. Now you, in him, will know my glory, and my life and you will show my glory to the watching world.

Trust these words. They are true. I will bring glory to my name through your life. Your most desperate circumstance, when given over to me, will give me glory. Your deepest heart ache, will result in my glory. Your sweetest victory, will result in my glory. As those in your life watch you, and you remain in me, they will see me. They will come to know me. They will find themselves drawn to my glory in you.

My beloved, look to me, lean into me, and when life presses hard against you, believe that I am for your good and will reveal the sweetest treasures to you, for my sake. My glory is your greatest reward. Your belief is the key ingredient to experience my glory. Be bold in your belief. Be quick to turn to me in trouble and victory. How great is the good I have in store for you, that I will bestow in the sight of all, for your good and my glory.

READING
178

What do you hear?

LIVE

How will you respond?

A prompt for living

Do you know someone who has faced a trial with courage? Do you know someone in the middle of difficulty? Take bold steps to encourage this person today. Give him or her courage to face the difficulty and pray that they would believe.

LISTEN
John 17:6-12

6 "I have revealed you to those whom you gave me out of the world. They were yours; you gave them to me and they have obeyed your word. 7 Now they know that everything you have given me comes from you. 8 For I gave them the words you gave me and they accepted them. They knew with certainty that I came from you, and they believed that you sent me. 9 I pray for them. I am not praying for the world, but for those you have given me, for they are yours. 10 All I have is yours, and all you have is mine. And glory has come to me through them. 11 I will remain in the world no longer, but they are still in the world, and I am coming to you. Holy Father, protect them by the power of your name, the name you gave me, so that they may be one as we are one. 12 While I was with them, I protected them and kept them safe by that name you gave me. None has been lost except the one doomed to destruction so that Scripture would be fulfilled."

READING
179

My beloved my eyes are ever on you. I know your goings out and when you arrive at home. I am familiar with all of your ways. Before a word is on your tongue I know it completely. I hem you in. Behind and before I have laid my hand upon. There is no where you can go where I am not. I am your shield. I am your home. I am your help. I am before you, behind you, and beside you. I hem you in! I am your protection.

I am keenly aware of my creation. My eye is on the largest of creatures and the smallest of atoms. I never will leave you, nor will I forsake you. I will never cast you from my presence.

As you walk through your day, thank me for my loving kindness and my sovereign care. As you walk through the valley, know that I am with you there too. As you walk to the highest peak of joy and the deepest place of sorrow, know that I am with you, I hold you, and I love you.

I am the most perfect Father. My care is beyond your human understanding, for no earthly father has ever come close to my perfect affection, attention and protection. In fact, many earthly fathers have clouded this vision of me. Sit for a moment in silence and imagine my loving arms surrounding you. I am with you. I will not abandon you. I am with you, even until the very end of the age.

What do you hear?

LIVE

How will you respond?

A prompt for living

Do you know someone who lives in fear? Take time to pray for him or her. Pray that they will know the steadfast love of God and that his/her life would know the peace that comes from belonging to Him.

13 "I am coming to you now, but I say these things while I am still in the world, so that they may have the full measure of my joy within them. 14 I have given them your word and the world has hated them, for they are not of the world any more than I am of the world. 15 My prayer is not that you take them out of the world but that you protect them from the evil one. 16 They are not of the world, even as I am not of it. 17 Sanctify them by the truth; your word is truth. 18 As you sent me into the world, I have sent them into the world. 19 For them I sanctify myself, that they too may be truly sanctified."

Trust that I am at work. Trust that though at times you are not understood by the world, that I am in you and leading you in my way. My son came and there were those who loved him and loved his way and loved his every word. There were also those who despised him. They rejected him. They hated his words and were overwhelmingly challenged by his way.

I know when you walk in the way of my Son that it is difficult. I know that it is an upstream swim. I know that it is difficult in every measure. But I also know, and smile as I think of it, that the way of my Son, the way of my kingdom is so good. It is rich and full and colorful. It is so incredibly beautiful that words cannot describe.

Trust my words. Even when you are ridiculed, trust my words. Even when you are rejected, trust my words. Even when it goes against the grain of the world, trust my words. Even when it makes no sense, trust my words. Trust, be not afraid. Trust and walk with me.

What do you hear?

LIVE

How will you respond?

A prompt for living

Is there a situation that you're in where you know to live out the way of Jesus would mean potential rejection? Invite some friends to pray with you and follow Jesus. Is there a person you've felt compelled to share the story of Jesus in your life? Invite some friends to pray with you and speak of Jesus.

LISTEN
John 17:20-23

20 "My prayer is not for them alone. I pray also for those who will believe in me through their message, 21 that all of them may be one, Father, just as you are in me and I am in you. May they also be in us so that the world may believe that you have sent me. 22 I have given them the glory that you gave me, that they may be one as we are one—23 I in them and you in me—so that they may be brought to complete unity. Then the world will know that you sent me and have loved them even as you have loved me."

It is my desire that all of those who believe in my Son would know perfect unity. Your belief in my Son unifies you with all others who believe. When this is true, why my child do you allow for differences to come among you? There are so many divisions between my children that are driven by pride and a belief that one has figured out the perfect way to understand and approach me. Every division among you is driven by pride. Every division among you will continue its dividing work as long as you believe your thinking is more advanced and complete than others.

The truth is, I am mystery. You can know me. You can approach me. You are able to have an intimate relationship with me, but you will never fully know the depth of my being and the exact make up of my character. This will always be true, for I did not create you to understand me, but to seek me. Creation can never understand the fullness of its Creator. This is truth. Therefore, I urge you my child, seek me completely, and hold your ideas of my truth with humility. Keep your heart and life open to all who say they follow the way of my Son.

My beloved created child, as you seek me, rejoice when others also seek after me. My glory is realized in you as you are unified with those who also seek me and my Son.

**What do
you hear?**

LIVE

**How will
you respond?**

**A prompt
for living**

Do you know someone who thinks of God, salvation, doctrine, and Jesus differently? When you find yourself judging that person, confess your pride and ask that person to coffee and get to know their story, as you get to know them, you may get to know Jesus a bit better too.

LISTEN
John 17:24

24 "Father, I want those you have given me to be with me where I am, and to see my glory, the glory you have given me because you loved me before the creation of the world."

You want to do for me. You painstakingly labor for the good you believe my kingdom needs. You weary yourself, thinking you are doing the good works required of my children. And yet you feel distant from me. You come to me, begging for my felt presence and I listen as I see you strive and work and toil.

I am not a cruel God who with holds himself from his beloved children. Nor am I cruel father who makes his children work to the bone to earn good standing, love, and affection.

It has always been and always will be my greatest desire to simply be with you. My son wanted you to be with him, to see the glory he holds, the glory I gave to him. Your work is often the noise that keeps you from my felt presence. You labor thinking it will earn you favor, when in fact, at times, your labor tells me you do not trust what I say is true.

You do not realize how often you work to earn. When you do this, you put a hand out, blocking my presence. Come to me, as you are, empty handed, broken, weary, and tired. Come to me, as you are, even in your pride, your accomplishment, your known provision. Come to me, and sit. Sit in the comfort of my presence, until your work, your thoughts, your ideas, your accomplishments become a distant murmur and all you hear is the loud silence of felt presence.

Come to me. Sit with me. Be with me. My love for you is deep. My love for you is without condition. My love for you is greater than all you could ask or imagine. Therefore, come. Come and lay all the noise of your work, all the guilt of your lack, all the pride of your accomplishment at my feet and sit in my love that is free. My glory will fall on you and you too will know that I have loved you from the beginning of time.

READING
182

What do you hear?

LIVE

How will you respond?

A prompt for living

Is there a great work you feel called to do? Is there a person you've been praying for, that they might know Jesus? Take some time today to come to Jesus and lay your ideas, call, friend, and work before him. Ask him to do the work of opening doors and bringing others to himself. Leave the work to God and sit in his presence, accepting the love he desires to give to you.

LISTEN
John 17:25-26

25 "Righteous Father, though the world does not know you, I know you, and they know that you have sent me. 26 I have made you known to them, and will continue to make you known in order that the love you have for me may be in them and that I myself may be in them."

I am not a secret god, nor am I a god who wishes to simply be mystery. I want you to know me. I want you to seek me. I want to reveal myself to you. I have given you many things to learn of me.

I have given you my Son. As you spend time with my Son you will know me, for he is my exact representation. It is through knowing him, that you will see me in many other places. Spend time with my Son. As you do, you will get to know me, for he knows me.

READING
183

I have given you vast creation that screams of my character. The very rhythm of the rivers, speak of my sovereignty. The birds and flowers show how detailed and creative I am. The grander of the mountains and the span of the seas shout of my majesty. From the tiniest cell to the largest animal, you will come to know Creator God with each encounter. Spend time in creation, and you will know me.

I have given you friendships. I have made you a relational people. In these relationships you will discover my heart for connection. Your longings to be connected to others speaks to the intimate God I am. I made you for relationship. Spend time with people, and you will know me.

Seek me and you will find me.
It is a promise that I always fulfill.

What do you hear?

LIVE

How will you respond?

A prompt for living

Make a point to have Jesus be a part of your every day interactions with people. Just like sharing about a great time you had with a friend, share about your time with Jesus and what you're thinking about and learning. If someone asked you how your morning was, and you spent time with Jesus, tell them . . . It was great, I start my day by reading from the teachings of Jesus and I learn from him all the time. If someone asks you what's new, tell them something you're learning.

Conversation about Jesus can be natural. You do not have to make a show of it. All you have to do is be fully you, and if Jesus is a part of you, then you get to share him as you offer your whole self to those around you.

JOHN 18 (Readings 184–192)

¹ When he had finished praying, Jesus left with his disciples and crossed the Kidron Valley. On the other side there was a garden, and he and his disciples went into it. ² Now Judas, who betrayed him, knew the place, because Jesus had often met there with his disciples. ³ So Judas came to the garden, guiding a detachment of soldiers and some officials from the chief priests and the Pharisees. They were carrying torches, lanterns, and weapons. ⁴ Jesus, knowing all that was going to happen to him, went out and asked them, "Who is it you want?" ⁵ "Jesus of Nazareth," they replied. "I am he," Jesus said. (And Judas the traitor was standing there with them.) ⁶ When Jesus said, "I am he," they drew back and fell to the ground.

Even when you turn from me, I come to you. Even when you betray me, I come to you. Even when you seek to destroy my name, I come to you.

My grace is sufficient for you. Even in the darkest hour, my grace will meet you there. Even when your heart turns away from me, my grace will meet you there. Even when your choices go against my hearts desires, my grace will meet you there. Even when your mind wanders and fixates on things contrary to my best, my grace will meet you there.

My love is beyond measure. Even when you despise your brother, my love will surround you. Even when you run from truth, my love will surround you. Even when you feel alone, my love will surround you. Even when your heart is tired, my love will meet you there.

My name, my grace, my love will come to you and you will fall to your knees as you are overwhelmed with the reality of my presence. Lean into my overwhelming presence and fall into my grace, love, and name.

**What do
you hear?**

LIVE

**How will
you respond?**

**A prompt
for living**

Do you hold a grudge? Is there someone you've said you'd never forgive? Today, ask Jesus to give you the courage to let go of the grudge, bitterness and tight gripped unforgiveness and free you to love this person again. Invite a friend to pray with you, write a letter to the person in need of forgiveness, or do something to symbolically let go and forgive.

LISTEN
John 18:7-9

> [7] *Again he asked them, "Who is it you want?" "Jesus of Nazareth," they said.* [8] *Jesus answered, "I told you that I am he. If you are looking for me, then let these men go."* [9] *This happened so that the words he had spoken would be fulfilled: "I have not lost one of those you gave me."*

I am good. I will always be good. Because of this, I will always be a God of my word. I will never speak a word or give a promise without the intent to make good of that which was spoken. I will fulfill what has been promised. . . . always.

This truth will be deeply challenged as you walk through life. From the very beginning this truth was challenged. In the garden, my loved children, were tested by the enemy of life. He lied to them, in essence telling them that I am not good and questioning my character and motivation. My very loved children believed this lie and they acted in response to the lie, rather than my truth.

You too are lied to daily. You are lied to more than once a day. You often engage these lies, forming beliefs about yourself, others and me based upon them. When the thought comes to mind that I am going to leave you stranded, return to me. I will never leave you nor will I forsake you. When the thought comes that I will disappoint you, return to me. I will give you the desires of your heart. When the thought comes that I will not accept you as you are, return to me. While you were yet a sinner, I sent my Son to die for you. When you are told you are not enough, return to me. It is my grace through faith; no amount of work will ever build a bridge to me.

I am good. I am good for you. I will always keep my word to you. Cling to my character and when a thought comes in, planting a contrary thought, return your thoughts to me. I am good and my love for you endures forever.

Reading

185

What do you hear?

LIVE

How will you respond?

A prompt for living

Today speak things that are true over those around you. When you see a person make a mistake, speak truth over them. When a person trips and falls, be the first to remind them that they are valuable. When a person fails, be the first to speak life over them. Your words are powerful, before you speak, think if these words give life or rob it. Then ask Jesus to give you truth to speak and do so!

LISTEN
John 18:10-11

¹⁰ Then Simon Peter, who had a sword, drew it and struck the high priest's servant, cutting off his right ear. (The servant's name was Malchus.) ¹¹ Jesus commanded Peter, "Put your sword away! Shall I not drink the cup the Father has given me?"

There are times when your life's circumstances prompt action in you that is not from me. Like Peter, you react instead of listen. You jump instead of look for my sovereign plan. You leap into action thinking it is to defend my name and my way when in truth your actions are contrary to what is best.

Remember that my way does not always make sense to you. There are times when the cup of suffering is a part of my divine plan. At times, even the way of the wicked, is such that their way will be a part of ushering in my kingdom purposes.

Before you react, stop, listen for my heart, and seek my will with a fervent persistence. You at times are to fight, while other times, you are to be silent. But in all things and in all circumstances, you are to trust that my plan is great and that I am in control. Trust that I am good and right and perfect and in every way I will bring about what is good and right and perfect. Entrust the immoralities of this world to me. Entrust the violence to me. Entrust the need for salvation to me. Allow your belief in me to increase and participate when I prompt you. In the same way, be still at my command, showing your submission to my sovereignty. You are not God, Savior, Healer, Protector, Provider, Defender, or Helper. I am. Entrust yourself to me and participate.

READING
186

What do you hear?

LIVE

How will you respond?

A prompt for living

Is there an issue in your world that angers you? Is it something to which you easily react? Next time you encounter this issue in conversation, through observation or in the media, take the issue to Jesus and ask him how you are to respond. If you are prompted to act, do so quickly. If you are told to be still, pray and entrust the issue to Jesus.

LISTEN
John 18:12-14

[12] Then the detachment of soldiers with its commander and the Jewish officials arrested Jesus. They bound him [13] and brought him first to Annas, who was the father-in-law of Caiaphas, the high priest that year. [14] Caiaphas was the one who had advised the Jewish leaders that it would be good if one man died for the people.

Things are not what they seem. I know that you feel the darkness of this world. I know that you feel as though the One Who Saves has been bound. I know that as you experience tragedy after tragedy, heart ache after heart ache and suffering beyond suffering that it feels as though I, your God has been bound. Do not allow this thought to capture you. Do not make an agreement with it.

I am a good God. In the midst of evil. I am a good God. In the midst of trial. I am a good God. In your time of distress. I am a good God. In your time of despair. I am a good God.

When it feels as though I've left you. I am with you, for I am a good God. When it seems as though all good has been overtaken by evil. I am with you, for I am a good God.

When it seems as though the war has been lost. I am with you, for I am a good God.

When darkness seems to suffocate you. I am light and I am with you, for I am a good God. When darkness clouds your day. I am light and I am with you, for I am a good God.

Things are not as they seem. The darkness will be destroyed by light. The night will shine like the day. Evil will bend its knee to Me! The King of Kings! Your distress is not out of my sight and it will not have victory over you. You are in me and I am in you and I have overcome the world. I have overcome. I have already won. In this dark hour, cling not to what you see, instead, cling to me. For I am light. I am with you. I am good.

**What do
you hear?**

LIVE

**How will
you respond?**

**A prompt
for living**

Use your words to speak life and hope over those in your life. Reach out to a friend in need, a co-worker, or a stranger in seeming distress and encourage them with truth.

LISTEN
John 18:15-18

15 Simon Peter and another disciple were following Jesus. Because this disciple was known to the high priest, he went with Jesus into the high priest's courtyard, 16 but Peter had to wait outside at the door. The other disciple, who was known to the high priest, came back, spoke to the servant girl on duty there and brought Peter in. 17 "You aren't one of this man's disciples too, are you?" she asked Peter. He replied, "I am not." 18 It was cold, and the servants and officials stood around a fire they had made to keep warm. Peter also was standing with them, warming himself.

You want those around you to be comfortable often more than you want them to know me. This is because you care too deeply about the opinion of others. You have handed your value to beggars and thieves and try to earn it back with your every move. You do not see this, but you live in this powerful reality. You work and dress and speak and withhold and serve and work out and strive so that you can earn value and acceptance from those around you.

You cannot earn value through what you own. You cannot earn value through those around you. You cannot earn value through your success. You cannot earn value through popularity or money. Earning value is a lie that leads you to destruction. You give out continually, only to end up feeling unacceptable and ashamed.

I gave you my Son so that in him you would have value. In my Son you are adopted into my royal family. Royalty is never earned, it is something you are born into. The same is true with me. You cannot earn value. NO! I give it to you as you are adopted into my family. This adoption is sealed and everlasting. It cannot be stolen from you. It cannot be lost.

Turn from your constant striving to earn the approval of others and believe. Believe that you are a child of a great king, for you are my child and your value can never be stolen.

READING

188

What do you hear?

LIVE

How will you respond?

A prompt for living

Pay attention this week to the names those around you call themselves. When a person puts him or herself down, speak life and identity over them. Maybe even take time to write a card to a person you know who has struggled to believe good about himself and encourage him!

19 Meanwhile, the high priest questioned Jesus about his disciples and his teaching. 20 "I have spoken openly to the world," Jesus replied. "I always taught in synagogues or at the temple, where all the Jews come together. I said nothing in secret. 21 Why question me? Ask those who heard me. Surely they know what I said." 22 When Jesus said this, one of the officials nearby slapped him in the face. "Is this the way you answer the high priest?" he demanded. 23 "If I said something wrong," Jesus replied, "testify as to what is wrong. But if I spoke the truth, why did you strike me?" 24 Then Annas sent him bound to Caiaphas the high priest.

When you are questioned because of me, because of my Son, do not fear. Yes, the world will not understand you and you will be tried because of me, but do not lose heart. I have overcome the world.

Though you do not know what lies ahead, trust me. Allow your steadfast belief in me be that which gives you the strength and fortitude to continue through whatever circumstances are before you. In every circumstance choose me. Choose my way.

When others come against you because of me, do not blame or look for a way out NO! Instead, choose me, choose my way, and hold tight to my truth as you respond to your accusers.

Do not be harsh or cruel, do not call names or seek vengeance. Do not take matters into your own hands. Even in the face of difficulty and ridicule for righteousness, choose me and choose my way. Ask me to rebuke evil, protect, and avenge; these are not your responsibility. They are mine alone.

I am with you, even until the very end of the age. Do not forget this promise.

READING
189

What do
you hear?

LIVE

How will
you respond?

A prompt
for living

Is there someone who has treated you unjustly because of your belief? Take some time to pray for that person. Pray that God would reveal himself to him. Pray that God would give you an opportunity to show His love to him. Pray that God would soften your heart towards him and that you would get to be a part of his salvation story.

LISTEN
John 18:25-27

25 Meanwhile, Simon Peter was still standing there warming himself. So they asked him, "You aren't one of his disciples too, are you?" he denied it, saying, "I am not." 26 One of the high priest's servants, a relative of the man whose ear Peter had cut off, challenged him, "Didn't I see you with him in the garden?" 27 Again Peter denied it, and at that moment a rooster began to crow.

My beloved, I know that you vacillate between finding your identity in me and finding it in the opinions of others. I know that you at times fear ridicule or worse. I know that you at times will seek to protect yourself, in your own human ways and understandings.

I do not shame you because of these things. I was not ashamed of Peter. I was sad for him. I watched as fear over came him and he reverted to a version of himself that sought after the approval of man. This internal motivation led him to deny my Son.

I watch as you also vacillate between finding your identity in me and finding your identity in the opinions of those who surround you. When this happens do not run from me. I am not ashamed of you. I will not shame you. I will not accuse you.

When you deny me, do what is contrary to human logic and run to me. Bring your fear, shame, and anxiety to me and allow me to remind you of your true self. Allow me to remind you of your true identity.

My beloved, do not fear man. Do not seek to appease or earn approval or value from them. Instead, rest in me. I am your good shepherd. I am your faithful Father. I am the lover of your soul and I will always receive you.

READING

190

What do you hear?

LIVE

How will you respond?

A prompt for living

Carry note cards with you. When come across an individual who is in need of hope or reminding of their value write a card and give it to him or her. It could be: a server at a restaurant who is having a bad day, a man or woman holding a sign asking for help, a co-worker, family member, grocery clerk. Ask God for words and write encouraging reminders of identity, then give the card to the person.

LISTEN
John 18:28–32

28 Then the Jewish leaders took Jesus from Caiaphas to the palace of the Roman governor. By now it was early morning, and to avoid ceremonial uncleanness they did not enter the palace, because they wanted to be able to eat the Passover. 29 So Pilate came out to them and asked, "What charges are you bringing against this man?" 30 "If he were not a criminal," they replied "we would not have handed him over to you." 31 Pilate said, "Take him yourselves and judge him by your own law." "But we have no right to execute anyone," they objected. 32 This took place to fulfill what Jesus had said about the kind of death he was going to die.

What do you hear?

I know what I am doing at all times. I know how every circumstance of the world fits into a larger picture. You have a small view. You work and labor to know the big picture, but you fall short. This is to protect you. You were not created to know the whole story at all times. The unfolding story of my creation and my way in the world is much larger and more beautiful and more profound than you could imagine.

What seems tragic to you may actually be beautiful. What may seem cruel may actually be compassion. What may seem unjust may actually be a part of a larger work of justice.

LIVE

Trust in me! Trust that I am sovereign.

How will you respond?

When you walk through the valley know that I am with you. Though the wind and the rain penetrate you, they will not take your life. When you walk through the fire, you will not be burned. I am your Holy One! I am your strength and shield. I am the one who is working all things together. Trust in me! Trust! Do not fear. Do not turn to doubt. Do not seek to make things work by human understanding and logic. Believe in me. Believe in my work and my way. Believe and watch as my story unfolds in the years of your life and beyond. Your life will be a part of the stories of faith for years to come.

Beloved, in the midst of your life circumstances, even those that do not make any sense . . . trust in me. I am your God and I am always for your good.

A prompt for living

Do you know someone in need of hope? Someone going through a rough season? Take some time today pray for them and then reach out to them. Let them know that you are praying and that you believe that God is good and will be good in their lives. Offer a small gift or reminder that they do not walk alone.

LISTEN
John 18:33-40

 33 Pilate then went back inside the palace, summoned Jesus and asked him, "Are you the king of the Jews?" 34 "Is that your own idea," Jesus asked, "or did others talk to you about me?" 35 "Am I a Jew?" Pilate replied. "Your own people and chief priests handed you over to me. What is it you have done?" 36 Jesus said, "My kingdom is not of this world. If it were, my servants would fight to prevent my arrest by Jewish leaders. But now my kingdom is from another place." 37 "You are a king, then!" said Pilate. Jesus answered, "You say that I am a king. In fact, the reason I was born and came into the world is to testify to the truth. Everyone on the side of truth listens to me." 38 "What is truth?" retorted Pilate. With this he went out again to the Jews gathered there and said, "I find no basis for a charge against him. 39 But it is your custom for me to release to you one prisoner at the time of the Passover. Do you want me to release 'the king of the Jews'?" 40 They shouted back, "No, not him! Give us Barabbas!" Now Barabbas had taken part in an uprising.

READING

192

Truth is the only language I speak. My lips have never known the taste of falsehood and no person has ever felt the sting of deception from me. My son came to testify to the truth. Any person who values truth believes in my Son, for he is, by nature, the very definition of truth. He is the way, the truth, and the life.

You search for truth in books, mentors, friends, and pastors. You seek for answers to be delivered by these individuals straight to you. Be careful my child when you do this! There are many who talk as though they belong to me, but do not. They like the sound of their own voices and desire for you to listen to them and heed only what they say. They give you advice for your ease and comfort, hoping to tickle your ears with half-truths and false promises. They are not acquainted with my good, for my good is beyond human understanding and is spoken by those who truly belong to me.

My sheep know my voice! Seek those who direct you to me. Seek me! My beloved I desire for you to experience life that is full and abundant and good, nothing less. Seek me! I promise that I will never lead you astray and I will never hand you over to the enemy. In fact, though you at times walk through the valley of the shadow of death, you do not have to fear the darkness, for I am with you and I will bless you right in front of your enemies. Trust in ME! Seek Me! Believe the words of my Son. Trust those who point you to him and you will know truth. You will know me.

What do you hear?

LIVE

How will you respond?

A prompt for living

When someone asks for your advice or thoughts today, before you say anything ask the person if they had consulted Jesus. Then take some time to pray before you speak. Ask Jesus to give you words and to speak through you truth.

JOHN 19   (Readings 193–202)

¹ Then Pilate took Jesus and had him flogged. ² The soldiers twisted together a crown of thorns and put it on his head. They clothed him in a purple robe and ³ went up to him again and again, saying, "Hail, king of the Jews!" And they slapped him in the face. ⁴ Once more Pilate came out and said to the Jews gathered there, "Look, I am brining him out to you to let you know that I find no basis for a charge against him." ⁵ When Jesus came out wearing the crown of thorns and the purple robe, Pilate said to them, "Here is the Man!" ⁶ As soon as the chief priest and their officials saw him, they shouted, "Crucify him! Crucify him!"

Even in the mocking words of those who spoke shame over my Son, they spoke the truth. My son is and was and always will be King. He was able to withstand the taunting words of those who sought to harm him because their words did not threaten his identity. For Him, his identity was never in question.

The question of identity rests in those who live in this world. You often find yourself struggling to believe truth and to find peace. You wrestle with pride and self-loathing as though you are on a teeter-totter, one moment you are connected with me, affirmed and secure and the next you fall prey to the whispers of the enemy of your soul.

You have been crucified with my Son and it is no longer you who live, but he lives in you. You share in a great heritage. You are a part of a royal lineage. You too, like Jesus, can withstand the taunting of the crowd to stand firm in your identity as a child of the most-high God. You are firm and secure.

May you live my dear child with the assurance that I am your Father. I have placed value on your head, you are mine! May this be the truth to which you hold and in this truth may you find great peace and humility.

What do you hear?

LIVE

How will you respond?

A prompt for living

Be a blessing today through an act of service. Go out of your way to serve someone today. Open doors, smile often, speak words of encouragement, give hope, and speak truth!

⁶ But Pilate answered, "You take him and crucify him. As for me, I find no basis for a charge against him." ⁷ The Jewish leaders insisted, "We have a law, and according to that law he must die, because he claimed to be the Son of God." ⁸ When Pilate heard this, he was even more afraid, ⁹ and he went back inside the palace. "Where do you come from?" he asked Jesus, but Jesus gave him no answer. ¹⁰ "Do you refuse to speak to me?" Pilate said. "Don't you realize I have power either to free you or to crucify you?" ¹¹ Jesus answered, "You would have no power over me if it were not given to you from above. Therefore the one who handed me over to you is guilty of a greater sin."

Greater is the one who is in you than anyone in the world. No spirit or person is greater than the one in whom you've found life. Believe in this. Trust that I am at work in you. Allow this to be the truth to which you hold in all circumstances. Give yourself to me completely and allow your belief to change your fear into peace, your pride into humility, your independence into dependence, your selfishness to selflessness, your anxiety into trust.

The one who is in you, actually holds you together, every ligament of you! The one who is in you formed the world and everything in it. Therefore, at my name every knee should bow and every tongue confess that my Son is the Lord! Believe this truth, there is no weapon that can stand against you!

READING
194

**What do
you hear?**

LIVE

**How will
you respond?**

**A prompt
for living**

Encourage a friend who is going through a difficult time.

LISTEN
John 19:12-16a

¹² From then on, Pilate tried to set Jesus free, but the Jewish leaders kept shouting, "If you let this man go, you are no friend of Caesar. Anyone who claims to be a king opposes Caesar." ¹³ When Pilate heard this, he brought Jesus out and sat down on the judge's seat at a place known as the Stone Pavement (which in Aramaic is Gabbatha). ¹⁴ It was the day of Preparation of the Passover; it was about noon. "Here is your king," Pilate said to the Jews. ¹⁵ But they shouted, "Take him away! Take him away! Crucify him!" "Shall I crucify your king?" Pilate asked. "We have no king but Caesar," the chief priests answered. ¹⁶ Finally Pilate handed him over to them to be crucified.

Be careful to not be misled in your belief about me. Be cautious in your understanding. The enemy would want nothing more than to deceive you and blind you to who I truly am. He lied to Adam and Eve, deceiving them about my identity and character, he deceived those who sought to crucify my Son as they did not recognize him as their king and he also wants to deceive you.

Be on guard. The enemy does seek to kill, steal, and destroy, but I am life, and all that is in me is good and right and perfect. I am life, I am light, in me there is no darkness at all. Trust this to be true. Trust that I am for your good and that I will always lead you in the way of life.

When you are tempted to believe that I am not good, or that I do not have good in store for you, immediately proclaim the truth that I am a good God. Be aware that good and comfortable are not the same thing. Be aware that my good often involves walking through the valley of the shadow of death. Walking through difficulty is not evidence that I am not a good God, when you walk in a difficult way turn to me, look for me and trust in me. I will be found when you look for me with all of your heart. You are my beloved.

READING

195

What do
you hear?

LIVE

How will
you respond?

A prompt
for living

Today ask Jesus to reveal to you that which is true and to show you where lies have taken root in the lives of those around you. When you see a lie, speak truth into it! Be a person who is generous with the beautiful, grace-filled, sometimes difficult, and always life-giving truth that comes from knowing God.

LISTEN
John 19:16b-18

16 So the soldiers took charge of Jesus. 17 Carrying his own cross, he went out to the place of the Skull (which in Aramaic is called Golgotha). 18 There they crucified him, and with him two others—one on each side and Jesus in the middle.

My beloved, I have always loved you. The ways others have treated me have never tempted me to stop loving them. My love is not attached to behavior. My love is not conditional. As I watched my Son carry his cross, where I knew he would suffer and where I knew he would die, I never lost sight of my love for you. Nor did my Son.

You worry about how you behave. You worry about what I'll think if you do this or that. You worry that my love will leave you if you do not perform with absolute perfection. You worry that if you do not serve well or give everything or avoid temptation and sin that I will strip my love from you. This is an impossibility. Every ounce of my love, that weighs more than the heavens and earth combined, is free and without condition. Therefore, neither life nor death, nor angels nor demons, nor things present nor things to come can separate you from my love.

Today, in your comings and goings, today, in your waking and in your sleeping, today, in your thinking, doing and feeling,-remember this truth. Remember that any good that comes from you is out of my love and never for it, for my love is not able to be purchased. If it were, it would cease to be love. Fall into this love and walk in it.

READING
196

What do you hear?

LIVE

How will you respond?

A prompt for living

Take some time to pray for your enemies. Pray for those whom you fear. Is it a people group? Is it a person? Is it religion? Pray! Pray for them to come to know Jesus and to be transformed by HIS love for them.

LISTEN
John 19:19-22

¹⁹ Pilate had a notice prepared and fastened to the cross. It read: Jesus of Nazareth, the King of the Jews. ²⁰ Many of the Jews read this sign, for the place where Jesus was crucified was near the city, and the sign was written in Aramaic, Latin and Greek. ²¹ The chief priests of the Jews protested to Pilate, "Do not write 'The King of the Jews,' but that this man claimed to be king of the Jews." ²² Pilate answered, "What I have written, I have written."

I am king. This fact does not change when one does not believe me to be such.

I am king.

I am a good king. I am the KING of all kings. Yes, my dear child I am good and I am king. These two truths are crucial to your life.

There will be many things that will invite you to believe that I am not good and there will be many things fighting for the place of king in your life. At times, you give the place of king to the opinions of others. At times you give kingship to your body. At times you give it to your work. Other times you give the place of king to society and the world around you. When you place anything as king over me you are placing your life under something that is not fully good. You are placing yourself under something that does not fully want you to experience, receive or live into good.

I am your good king. Place yourself under my good and pure and righteous kingship. Share in my kingdom. Come to me, your good king, and I will guide you all of your days.

READING
197

What do you hear?

LIVE

How will you respond?

A prompt for living

Pray for five people today who you would like to experience God as a good King. If you have an idea to encourage or be kind to them, do it!

²³ When the soldiers crucified Jesus, they took his clothes, dividing them into four shares, one for each of them, with the undergarment remaining. This garment was seamless, woven in one piece from top to bottom. ²⁴ "Let's not tear it," they said to one another. "Let's decide by lot who will get it." This happened that the scripture might be fulfilled that said, "They divided my clothes among them and cast lots for my garment." So this is what the soldiers did.

It is too often that you only want what I will give you more than you want me. I am the greatest gift. I alone am enough. But, you get caught up in what I can do and what I can give. Your longings become your idols and you beg and plead with me to release what you see as blessing over you.

My beloved, I long for you to simply want me, to know that I am enough, that I am the ultimate gift. I long for you to love me, simply because I am your good King and not for any other reason. I want your heart. The whole thing. I want you. All of you. You are the greatest offering of worship.

My beloved child, know that I care so deeply for you and I alone am your portion. I am your provision. May you be encouraged as you walk in me and may you know the transformation that occurs when you seek me with all of your heart.

What do you hear?

LIVE

How will you respond?

A prompt for living

Today offer yourself to the Lord and obey every prompting to do good in response to His voice.

25 Near the cross of Jesus stood his mother, his mother's sister, Mary the wife of Clopas, and Mary Magdalene. 26 When Jesus saw his mother there, and the disciple whom he loved standing nearby, he said to her, "Woman, here is your son," 27 and to the disciple, "Here is your mother." From that time on, this disciple took her into his home.

My way is a way of completion, in every detail. There are times where you feel the pain and sting of loss, do not fret, I did not forget you in the midst of your loss. Do not for one second believe that I have robbed you of anything. I am a God who gives and who takes away, but neither the giving nor the taking is done without intension and both are done for your good and the good of others.

When you feel grief, look for my provision.

When you know loss, look for what is found.

When you experience the death of a dream, look for life around you.

When you walk through the valley, expect the mountain.

When you feel rejection, look for places of acceptance.

When you experience pain, look for places of peace.

When you know a deep and profound stripping, look for what is being added.

When something is taken for your good there will always be provision in the midst.

One does not happen without the other. But you must look. Looking is a matter of belief. It is the belief that I am good and right and perfect and that I will always lead you in the way of life.

What do you hear?

LIVE

How will you respond?

A prompt for living

Do you know someone who is going through a trial? Do you have a friend or co-worker who is experiencing loss? Ask Jesus how you might encourage them. Do the good that comes to mind. Then you, may just be a part of the good in the midst of the painful!

LISTEN
John 19:28–30

28 Later, knowing that everything had now been finished, and so that Scripture would be fulfilled, Jesus said, "I am thirsty." 29 A jar of wine vinegar was there, so they soaked a sponge in it, put the sponge on a stalk of hyssop plant, and lifted it to Jesus' lips. 30 When he had received the drink, Jesus said, "It is finished." With that, he bowed his head and gave up his spirit.

I am a God of completion. So often you believe that I am a god of partiality. I have heard your prayers. I know the longings of your heart. I know the pain you feel and the lies and agreements you've made with the enemy of life. I know that to which you have fell victim. I am listening. I am answering. As I answer and rescue and redeem it is not yours to work or strive. I am Savior, you need only be still.

Your striving is evidence of the fact that your belief has not yet taken over. Your striving is your way of picking up where you feel as though I've left off. Your striving is the manifestation of your unbelief.

My names hold the truth of my promise. I am Savior, Provider, Healer, Redeemer, Life, Light, Rescue, Present, and Truth. I will be complete in all things. I will never start to heal you only to forget you. I will never start to provide for you only to leave you hanging. I will never start a saving process only to hand you over to the enemy. I will never lead you to life only to drop you off at death's doorstep. Believe in me. Believe that I am complete in all things—all of the time. Come to me, I will give you rest as I who began a good work in you will be faithful to complete it.

What do you hear?

LIVE

How will you respond?

A prompt for living

Think of a person in your life who is experiencing a difficulty or is going through a transformative process. Send them a card or a small gift that is a reminder that God is complete and will be faithful to see the process through to completion.

³¹ Now it was the day of Preparation, and the next day was to be a special Sabbath. Because the Jewish leaders did not want the bodies left on the crosses during the Sabbath, they asked Pilate to have the legs broken and the bodies taken down. ³² The soldiers therefore came and broke the legs of the first man who had been crucified with Jesus, and then those of the other. ³³ But when they came to Jesus and found that he was already dead, they did not break his legs. ³⁴ Instead, one of the soldiers pierced Jesus' side with a spear, bringing a sudden flow of blood and water. ³⁵ The man who saw it has given testimony, and his testimony is true. He knows that he tells the truth, and he testifies so that you also may believe. ³⁶ These things happened so that the scripture would be fulfilled: "Not one of his bones will be broken," ³⁷ and, as another scripture says, "They will look on the one they have pierced."

READING

201

I know this season doesn't make sense. To you, it appears that death has won and it won quickly. To you, all of these events of your life seem to bring darkness apart from me. Oh, my dear child, know that my view is much longer. It is in my view that words spoken long before are a part of now. The words give context to now, to today. The events of today, will collide with events to come and there, you too will find me and realize my faithfulness in a deep and true way.

Do not hide your grief. Do not fear the events in which you find yourself. Instead, bring your complaints to me, your trusting and loving Father, and I will walk with you. I am with you in your living, your sorrow, your unmet desires, your emptiness and your places of overflowing joy. I am your source and the one who holds the entirety of your story. Be at peace, your journey has my approval. Be at peace, I am near. Be at peace, I know the whole. Be at peace, in the now. Trust me, the one who has the long view and walk in my peace.

What do you hear?

LIVE

How will you respond?

A prompt for living

Is there a person in your life who is making choices that rub you the wrong way?
Take time to pray for them and ask God to give you a long view for that individual's story.
Seek to encourage the person in some way, a card, call, text, email, meal or coffee . . .
whatever it may be, do something to encourage the person as you pray.

38 Later, Joseph of Arimathea asked Pilate for the body of Jesus. Now Joseph was a disciple of Jesus, but secretly because he feared the Jewish leaders. With Pilate's permission, he came and took the body away. 39 He was accompanied by Nicodemus, the man who earlier had visited Jesus at Night. Nicodemus brought a mixture of myrrh and aloes, about seventy-five pounds. 40 Taking Jesus' body, the two of them wrapped it, with the spices, in the strips of linen. This was in accordance with Jewish burial customs. 41 At the place where Jesus was crucified, there was a garden, and in the garden a new tomb, in which no one had ever been laid. 42 Because it was the Jewish day of Preparation and since the tomb was nearby, they laid Jesus there.

I see your struggle to put the opinions of others before me. I see how at times you hold back your expressive love for me out of fear of what others will think. I know that you strive and work hard to do what is right in the eyes of man. I know. Come out of hiding. You are acceptable. You are seen. You are loved. You are chosen. You are mine.

Believe these words with active belief. Believe that my love for you covers you and washes over you in grace. I meet you in the garden, just as my Son was carried to the garden and just as Adam and Eve met with me in the garden. The garden is the place of life and death. It is the place where new life begins and the enemy will be destroyed. Though you have listened to the lies of the enemy that your value is given to you by the opinions of others, believe that lie no more. Step into a new story, bury the story of death and come out.

Come to me. Come and receive. Come, take off those burial clothes, take off the fig leaves you've used to cover yourself, the unacceptability found in your once unnoticeable nakedness, and bury with my Son the shame that has kept you from me.

READING
202

What do you hear?

LIVE

How will you respond?

A prompt for living

Intimacy with others is built as we share our truest (naked) selves with them. Is there a friend with whom you'd like to build a deeper connection? Take the risk to share your story.

John 20 (Readings 203–208)

LISTEN
John 20:1-10

¹ Early on the first day of the week, while it was still dark, Mary Magdalene went to the tomb and saw that the stone had been removed from the entrance. ² So she came running to Simon Peter and the other disciple, the one Jesus loved, and said, "They have taken the Lord out of the tomb, and we don't know where they have put him!" ³ So Peter and the other disciple started for the tomb. ⁴ Both were running, but the other disciple outran Peter and reached the tomb first. ⁵ He bent over and looked in at the strips of linen lying there but did not go in. ⁶ Then Simon Peter came along behind him and went straight into the tomb. He saw the strips of linen lying there, ⁷ as well as the cloth that had been wrapped around Jesus' head. The cloth was still lying in its place, separate from the linen. ⁸ Finally the other disciple, who had reached the tomb first, also went inside. He saw and believed. ⁹ (They still did not understand from Scripture that Jesus had to rise from the dead." ¹⁰ Then the disciples went back to where they were staying.

My ways are not your ways. My thoughts are not your thoughts. Your imagination is so small. I speak of great things, but you do not recognize them for you have limited understanding. I am the God of the impossible. I can do all things. I do not make bold statements without purpose or intension. I will do all that I have said. Believe! Believe!

I will rescue you from within the fire. I will heal you, before you know you're well. I will allow the death to creep and then life to shine in like the brightest light. I will provide from nothing. I will bring hope from despair. I will bring joy from grief. I will bring life from death. Trust this. Believe in me. I will do more than you can ask or imagine. Do not limit me to your understanding, but step out of the fear of the unknown, the what ifs, the if onlys, and the places where never, always, only, and impossible are the words used to describe. Step into healing, relationship, resurrection, and good. Allow your movement, your silence, your stillness, and your action to be your belief.

What do you hear?

LIVE

How will you respond?

A prompt for living

Live in such a way that you say, "yes" to Jesus and believe with action for yourself and others. Give courage to those around you who need belief.

11 Now Mary stood outside the tomb crying. As she wept, she bent over to look into the tomb 12 and saw two angels in white, seated where Jesus' body had been, one at the head and the other at the foot. 13 They asked her, "Woman, why are you crying?" "They have taken my Lord away," she said, "and I don't know where they have put him." 14 At this, she turned around and saw Jesus standing there, but she did not realize that it was Jesus. 15 He asked her, "Woman, why are you crying? Who is it you are looking for?" Thinking he was the gardener, she said, "Sir, if you have carried him away, tell me where you have put him, and I will get him." 16 Jesus said to her, "Mary." She turned toward him and cried out in Aramaic, "Rabooni!" (which means "teacher")

The impossible is not out of reach. Impossible is a concept known to man, but not to me. For, to me, nothing is impossible. Your imagination can reach only so far. Though I have told you I am the resurrection and the life, you believe only in the idea, not the reality. The reality seems too good to be true.

Believing that the impossible is possible, that joy can be real and that longings can be fulfilled is a deep fear of yours. Believing, in your mind, leads to disappointment. Questions rise, riddled with doubt: How can this be?

What if God doesn't? How will He ever? He won't do that for me? I've prayed and no mountain has been moved.

Even when mountains stand still and sickness makes its way to death's door, believe that I, who am God, is capable of more than you can ask or imagine. My ways are not your ways and my thoughts are not your thoughts. Believe. Trust. Step. Step into the impossible, even before the impossible reveals its way to possible. My love for you is deep and I am working in every situation for your good. Believe and receive.

What do you hear?

LIVE

How will you respond?

A prompt for living

Choose one friend with whom you can share the impossibility that you'd like to see made possible. Ask him/her to do the same. After you share, pray with one another that you would believe and live in that belief, even if circumstantially things have not changed.

LISTEN
John 20:17-18

17 Jesus said, "Do not hold on to me, for I have not yet ascended to the Father. Go instead to my brothers and tell them, 'I am ascending to my Father and your Father, to my God and your God.'" 18 Mary Magdalene went to the disciples with the news: "I have seen the Lord!" And she told them that he had said these things to her.

I am a God of abundant good. I am not holding out on my children. I am not a god of empty promises nor am I a god who hides himself. You do not see because you do not know me. You do not hear because you do not know my word. You do not understand because you do not seek me.

My name is Savior, Provider, Redeemer.

My name is Mighty, Enthroned One, Creator.

My name is Holy, Sovereign, All Powerful One.

My name is Beauty, Grace, and Love.

My name is Good.

These are only a glimpse of my names. These hold only part of who I am. When you see or experience these, you taste in the smallest way, me. You see me. You see evidence of me in my character being expressed in your every day.

My word does not return void. It is powerful and effective. It is sweet. It is story. It is truth, alive, and active. It is sharper than any sword. My word is yours to hear. Read it and listen. You will hear me speak through it. You will hear me invite you, encourage you, and correct you. When you read, you will hear. When you remember it and hide it in your heart you will carry it with you and I will speak to you from it every day.

I will give you understanding, sight, and hearing as you seek me. This is my promise. Remember and live in that today, then go and tell of all you have seen and heard.

What do you hear?

LIVE

How will you respond?

A prompt for living

Host a dinner party for a small group of friends. At some point during dinner ask people how they have experienced beauty/good/light or love in the past year. Use that as a starting point for conversation about the Lord.

LISTEN
John 20:19-23

19 On the evening of that first day of the week, when the disciples were together, with the doors locked for fear of the Jewish leaders, Jesus came and stood among them and said, "Peace be with you!" 20 After he said this, he showed them his hands and side. The disciples were overjoyed when they saw the Lord. 22 Again Jesus said, "Peace be with you! As the Father has sent me, I am sending you." 22 And with that he breathed on them and said, "Receive the Holy Spirit. 23 If you forgive anyone's sins, their sins are forgiven; if you do not forgive them, they are not forgiven."

My friends I give you peace. I leave my peace. I breathe on you and peace fills the room as my Spirit fills your lungs. Peace. It comes from surrender to me. Peace comes when you allow me to be the source of all of you. When I am the very air in your lungs, all of life can be met with my peace and forgiveness is easily given. When you know me, when you remain in me, when you breathe in my Spirit, My peace is given to you, and you are free to live and love and give and relate.

In your life, you will have trouble. You will be hurt. Your heart will be broken. People will let you down. People will allow their fear to drive them more than my truth and your heart will feel the sting of rejection. When you do, when life seems to wash over you like a tidal wave, breathe me in, and know my peace! It is here for you.

Do not hand yourself to vengeance, self-righteousness, entitlement, and the like. These will only lead you away from me. Instead, go in the opposite direction. When war breaks out, walk away from it. When people yell, reach out a hand of help. When your heart is broken, love the one who caused its pain. By these actions, people will know that you belong to me, and my peace will be passed on to another.

What do you hear?

LIVE

How will you respond?

A prompt for living

Is there someone in your life who has hurt you, caused pain, betrayed you in some way? Do something today to bless them. Even if they never know, bless them with your prayers, the way you speak of them and how you treat their memory in your own spirit. Bless.

24 Now Thomas (also known as Didymus), one of the Twelve, was not with the disciples when Jesus came. 25 So the other disciples told him, "We have seen the Lord!" But he said to them, "unless I see the nail marks in his hands and put my finger where the nails were, and put my hand into his side, I will not believe." 26 A week later his disciples were in the house again, and Thomas was with them. Though the doors were locked, Jesus came and stood among them and said, "Peace be with you!" 27 Then he said to Thomas, "Put your finger here; see my hands. Reach out your hand and put it into my side. Stop doubting and believe." 28 Thomas said to him, "My Lord and my God!" 29 Then Jesus told him, "Because you have seen me, you have believed; blessed are those who have not seen and yet have believed."

Your doubt does not bewilder me. When doubt moves you toward my Son it is evidence of a desire for faith. It is this kind of doubt that leads you to closer relationship with me. For doubt, when held humbly, is the catalyst for greater knowledge and understanding, and an impetus for greater intimacy with me. When your doubt is spoken it is revealed as nakedness. Know that your doubts, your longings, and your unmet desires are not hidden from my sight. Speak of these things. Speak of your fears and be released from their stronghold. When you seek me with your doubt, you will find your doubt being met with evidence of that which is true. For I love to be found by my children.

Do not hide your doubt from me. Doubt that is hidden leads you away from me. When you clothe your doubt in disbelief, anger, pride, resentment or arrogant knowledge you are actually hiding, and hiding, always leads to felt disconnection from me. Come out of hiding! Speak your doubt and I will turn your doubt to greater belief. The humbly exposed doubt of the seeker, will lead to belief and connection, this I promise you.

What do you hear?

LIVE

How will you respond?

A prompt for living

Listen to the doubts of a friend. Hold their doubts as questions and allow the doubt to lead you toward Jesus. Do not shun a person for doubting, but instead, welcome them and their questions. Do this by listening, caring, and responding to their doubt with your belief, acceptance, and love.

LISTEN
John 20:30–31

30 Jesus performed many other signs in the presence of his disciples, which are not recorded in this book. 31 But these are written that you believe that Jesus is the Messiah, the Son of God, and that by believing you may have life in his name.

It is my desire that you have life. Because I love you, I want what is best for you. I am not a controlling God, simply because I like the control, that is a human idea. I am a loving God who desires all people to thrive, to live well, to know love, and to be free. Morality is a human idea. It comes from a place of controlling behavior for the sake of being right.

I am beyond morality.

I am a God whose very name is love. Every single thing I do. Every single idea that I have. Every single word that I speak is driven by and is found in love, for love is my only language.

Reading
208

I do desire that all will come to belief in my Son. This is because I love you. This is because I love all of humanity.

You do not know the way of love. Your mind is small and your understanding is so limited. Your idea of love is base only upon a comfortable human experience. The purest form of love follows in the way of Jesus and leads to complete freedom; freedom to live wholly in my way. I know this is difficult for you, because you have used rules to control, you have used belief to manipulate. You have been wounded by those who misuse my name or the name of my Son to gain power. The enemy of love and life is hard at work to rob all people, everywhere from belief in my Son. He has proposed a false idea of love, based in human comfort and happiness. This understanding will ultimately lead toward death.

My child, my beloved, live in my love. Seek it out. Search for it. IT is like a treasure hidden in a field, when one knows how great the treasure is he will sell all that he has to buy the field. My love is my kingdom. My son is the very picture of this love. Believe! Believe in this love and walk in it, root yourself in it, and be free.

What do you hear?

LIVE

How will you respond?

A prompt for living

Ask God to increase your love for those around you. Ask Him to show you how you might love others well. When an idea comes to mind how you might love someone around you, put the idea to action . . . do not wait!

John 21 (Readings 209–215)

LISTEN
John 21:1-3

¹ Afterward Jesus appeared again to his disciples, by the Sea of Galilee. It happened this way: ² Simon Peter, Thomas (also known as Didymus), Nathanael from Cana in Galilee, the sons of Zebedee, and two other disciples were together. ³ "I'm going out to fish," Simon Peter told them, and they said, "We'll go with you." So they went out and got into the boat, but that night they caught nothing.

When life feels impossible, you run to what you know. You return to what is comfortable. You turn back to the possible. Yes, at times life feels so impossible that it seems impossible to trust. In these times know that I am very present. I am at work. I have not abandoned you to impossibility. I am with you. I am doing a good thing. It is when I have taken you beyond what you know how to ask or imagine that I reveal to you the unimaginable.

Mary and Martha could imagine that my Son could heal their brother, they had no imagination that he could be brought back to life. Those who were closest with my Son had no imagination for their lives after all that had transpired with my Son. Therefore, they returned to what they knew.

Look for me in the impossible. Trust that I am leading and present. Give ear to my words and seek me and find me. When tempted to return to the possible, continue to walk in belief, knowing that I am with you. And will be, even to the end of the age.

READING
209

What do you hear?

LIVE

How will you respond?

A prompt for living

Do you have a friend or family member in an incredibly impossible situation? Take time to listen, to let them know they are not alone and to pray with them.

LISTEN
John 21:4-7a

⁴ Early in the morning, Jesus stood on the shore, but the disciples did not realize that it was Jesus. ⁵ He called out to them, "Friends haven't you any fish?" "No," they answered. ⁶ He said, "Throw your net on the right side of the boat and you will find some." When they did, they were unable to haul the net in because of the large number of fish. ⁷ Then the disciple whom Jesus loved said to Peter, "It is the Lord!"

I am the God of the third way. You see your circumstances through the lens of two options, the one you can imagine and the one of nothing, failure, end, deprivation, and grief. I am the God of the third way. I am the God who is always working to bring about good and the miraculous, not by what you see, but by what you don't see.

Do not let your circumstances dictate what is possible for yourself or others. Instead look for me, listen to me, and obediently follow my way. I will speak and give you an option. Pray. Seek Me. Follow after what I say. Be willing to let your nets down on the other side of the boat and do so, believing that I will meet you there. When you step into the third way, you will see me. You will recognize that I'm working, and you will point others to me with the story of your life. Do not fear. Do not despair. Believe. Step. and Receive.

What do you hear?

LIVE

How will you respond?

A prompt for living

Do you have a friend going through a very difficult season, challenge, or circumstance? Get together with them, gather a group of trusted friends and pray to the Lord. Together, ask Jesus what he wants you to see and to reveal a third way. Seek the Lord together and step in obedience to what he says.

LISTEN
John 21:7b-12a

⁷ As soon as Simon Peter heard him say, It is the Lord," he wrapped his outer garment around him (for he had taken it off) and jumped into the water. ⁸ The other disciples followed in the boat, towing the net full of fish, for they were not far from shore, about a hundred yards. ⁹ When they landed, they saw a fire of burning coals there with fish on it, and some bread. ¹⁰ Jesus said to them, "Bring some of the fish you have just caught." ¹¹ So Simon Peter climbed back into the boat and dragged the net ashore. It was full of large fish, 153, but even with so many the net was not torn. ¹² Jesus said to them "Come and have breakfast."

I am your provision. I am your portion. I set food on your table and I allow for the big catch. All provision is mine, from every angle . . . provision is mine. Do not fret about what you should eat or what you should drink. Do not worry about what you are to wear. These worries rob you from joy and steal from you my presence.

My dear one, I love you. I see your heart ache. I know you wonder how you will accomplish all before you. I feel the pounding of your heart as you think of your need. I care about these things. I have invited you to life with me and as you walk with me, you will know that I am your portion, help, and provision. As you walk with me you will know that not a meal appears on the table without my grace. When your pay check arrives, thank me, for I am your ultimate provider. Not a gift in your life comes separate from me, for every good and perfect gift comes from me. When you see that I am your provider and you live in that faith your worry will subside and you will walk in the truth of my help.

Confess your worry. Say aloud your complaint. Shout your discomfort. Then thank me, for though you may not see it, I am providing for you. Lean into faith, allow for deep belief to well up within you and listen for my voice. Trust and obey. Trust and do not fear.

And when the provision comes, thank me for I am your generous provider.

What do you hear?

LIVE

How will you respond?

A prompt for living

Ask God to increase your love for those around you. Ask Him to show you how you might love others well. When an idea comes to mind how you might love someone around you, put the idea to action . . . do not wait!

LISTEN
John 21:12b-14

12 Jesus said to them, "Come and have breakfast." None of the disciples dared ask him, "Who are you?" They knew it was the Lord. 13 Jesus came, took the bread and gave it to them, and did the same with the fish. 14 This was now the third time Jesus appeared to his disciples after he was raised from the dead.

Come. It is my constant invitation for you and I never invite you to come without your good in mind. Come, follow me. Come, and eat. Come out of hiding. Come.

My beloved, you are mine and though you return to your former ways, though you walk away from me, though you believe that you have discovered a better way, though you know separation from me, my invitation is always the same. Come. Come to me.

I am your provider. Trust and come.

I am your help. Believe and come.

I am your hope. Receive and come.

I am your salvation. Breathe and come.

I am your shepherd. Walk and come.

I am your way. Step and come.

I am your truth. Have faith and come.

I am your life source. Soak in it and come.

Come to me, you who are weary, you who are tired, you who are afraid, you who know shame, you who have sinned, you who don't believe, you who are in hiding—Come to me.

What do you hear?

LIVE

How will you respond?

A prompt for living

Next time a friend asks your advice or is going through crisis, take a moment and to remind your friend of the invitations of Jesus to come to him. Then, with your friend, respond to the invitation and come to Jesus together, in prayer, in belief, in response.

15 When they had finished eating, Jesus said to Simon Peter, "Simon son of John, do you love me more than these?" "Yes, Lord," he said, "you know that I love you." Jesus said, "Feed my lambs." 16 Again Jesus said, "Simon son of John, do you love me?" He answered, "Yes, Lord, you know that I love you." Jesus said, " Take care of my sheep." 17 The third time he said to him, " Simon son of John, do you love me?" Peter was hurt because Jesus asked him the third time, "Do you love me?" He said, "Lord, you know all things; you know that I love you." Jesus said, "Feed my sheep. 18 Very truly I tell you, when you were younger you dressed yourself and went where you wanted; but when you are old you will stretch out your hands, and someone else will dress you and lead you where you do not want to go." 19 Jesus said this to indicate the kind of death by which Peter would glorify God. Then he said to him, "Follow me!"

READING

213

Your love for me is evidenced by your following in the way of my Son. At times you love your work, your security, your comfort, your home, your friends, your life more than me. It is imperative that you completely give yourself to me and entrust all of you to me. When you lose your life in me, you actually find it.

My child, I know that all you hold and value are significant. I know that the choices before you feel paramount. I know that your work feels like the most important thing. Do not be fooled. All of this every choice, every piece of work, every cause, every relationship is a gift and you, my child must follow my Son in all of these things. You must listen and respond to him. You must follow him. His way will always lead to life. When you love these things more than me, they will be your god and your life will evidence the god of your choice.

I am love. When I am your God, your life will evidence love both in your receptivity of my love and in your giving of love to others. Follow me, for I am good and right and perfect. I am love.

What do you hear?

LIVE

How will you respond?

A prompt for living

Take stock of all that you follow. Do you follow the way of work? The way of the opinions of others? The way of money? The way of success? When you have realized all that you follow, take time to reorient yourself around me and my way of love. Then, go out of your way to love others, because you know first my love for you.

LISTEN
John 21:20-24

20 Peter turned and saw that the disciple whom Jesus loved was following them. (This was the one who had leaned back against Jesus at the supper and had said, "Lord, who is going to betray you?") 22 When Peter saw him, he asked, "Lord, what about him?" 22 Jesus answered, "If I want him to remain alive until I return, what is that to you? You must follow me." 23 Because of this, the rumor spread among the believers that this disciple would not die. But Jesus did not say that he would not die; he only said, "If I want him to remain alive until I return, what is that to you?" 24 This is the disciple who testifies to these things and who wrote them down. We know that his testimony is true.

My child you compare your life to those of others. You imagine I do all things the same, for all of those that I love. I am a God of grace. I am a God of complete mercy. I am a God who is good, who is right and who is perfect. I know you, for I made you.

It is not for you to compare your life with the lives of others. It is not yours to question my good because I didn't do this or that the same way I did such things in the lives of those around you. I know the good you need. I know the depth of your heart's cry. I know the best for you. When you compare and question, you evidence a distrust in me and my way. But, when you know my love for you is perfect, you will fear nothing, for you believe that I am for you.

And when I, the King of all the earth, am for you, who can ever be against you? What circumstance is too big for me?

Trust in me. Trust in my divine nature. Trust in my sovereign power. Trust in my good for you. Trust and keep walking. Allow my love for you be that which carries you.

READING
214

What do you hear?

LIVE

How will you respond?

A prompt for living

The next time someone around you is comparing his or her life to that of another, encourage them to trust the Lord and His good for their life today. Be a witness to His good in your life and story.

LISTEN
John 21:25

²⁵ Jesus did many other things as well. If every one of them were written down, I suppose that even the whole world would not have room for the books that would be written.

I am always at work.

I am the God for whom impossible is not a word. I am the God of life. I am the God of hope. I am the God of good. I am the God of truth. I am the God of forgiveness. I am the God who saves. I am the God who sees. I am the God who is above all things. I am the God of light. I am the God of beauty. I am the God of restoration. I am the God who rebuilds. I am the God who restores. I am the God who blesses. I am the God who loves. I am the God of rescue. I am all powerful. I am all knowing. I am so very faithful.

I am the God of life. I am the God of insurmountable riches. I am the God who heals. I am the God who gives. I am the God who also takes away. I am the very way. I am the God of compassion and comfort. I am the God of grace. I am the God of mercy. I am the God who provides. I am the God brings life from that which is dead. I am the God of joy. I am the God who is faithful. I am God. I alone am He.

There are not enough pages in the world to hold the works of my hand in your life. Believe. Believe and receive.

Reading

215

What do you hear?

LIVE

How will you respond?

A prompt for living

Tell one story daily of the goodness of God in your life. Look for ways to declare Him, to tell his story, and to reflect His character. May your daily life be the evidence of a God who is good and who is good for you, every single day.